Persons in Community

Persons in Community
African Ethics in a Global Culture

EDITED BY
RONALD NICOLSON

UNIVERSITY OF KwaZulu-Natal PRESS

Published in 2008 by University of KwaZulu-Natal Press
Private Bag X01
Scottsville 3209
South Africa
E-mail: books@ukzn.ac.za
Website: www.ukznpress.co.za

© 2008 University of KwaZulu-Natal

All rights reserved. No part of this publication may be reproduced or transmitted in any form or by any means, electronic or mechanical, including photocopying, or recording on any information storage and retrieval system, without prior permission in writing from the publishers.

ISBN: 978-1-86914-133-2

Managing editor: Sally Hines
Editor: Alison Lockhart
Typesetting: Patricia Comrie
Indexer: Brenda Williams-Wynn
Cover design: Flying Ant Designs
Cover photograph: Courtesy of SA Tourism

Printed and bound by Interpak Books, Pietermaritzburg

Contents

Introduction
  Persons in Community: *Ubuntu* in the Global Village 1
    RONALD NICOLSON

Chapter 1
  African Ethics in a Globalising World 15
    AUGUSTINE SHUTTE

Chapter 2
  Ubuntu and Harmony: An African Approach
  to Morality and Ethics 35
    NHLANHLA MKHIZE

Chapter 3
  Religious Ethics, HIV and AIDS and Masculinities
  in Southern Africa 45
    EZRA CHITANDO

Chapter 4
  Reflections on Reconciliation and *Ubuntu* 65
    R. NEVILLE RICHARDSON

Chapter 5
  On African Ethics and the Appropriation of Western Capitalism:
  Cultural and Moral Constraints to the Evolution of Capitalism
  in Post-colonial Africa 85
    MUNYARADZI FELIX MUROVE

Chapter 6
  Ethics, African Societal Values and the Workplace 111
    JOHN MTYUWAFHETHU MAFUNISA

Chapter 7
 Africa's Healing Wisdom: Spiritual and Ethical Values
 of Traditional African Healthcare Practices 125
  LUCINDA DOMOKO MANDA

Contributors 141
Index 143

The financial support and moral encouragement for this project from the Unilever Foundation for Education and Development and the Atlantic Philanthropies are gratefully acknowledged – without their help, this project could not have happened.

INTRODUCTION

Persons in Community
Ubuntu in the Global Village

RONALD NICOLSON

THE AFRICAN ETHICS Initiative, which is part of the Unilever Ethics Centre at the University of KwaZulu-Natal, commissioned this book. The Ethics Centre as a whole is committed to the study of all ethical traditions – philosophical, religious and cultural – to see what common light they can cast on the practical and applied ethical issues that face southern Africa and the rest of the world. The intention of the African Ethics Initiative within the Centre is to research, clarify and highlight the contributions of ethics derived from sub-Saharan African culture and lived experience as part of the panorama of rich ethical guidance from which we may draw.

This book began in 2004, when the African Ethics Initiative called together a group of eminent scholars of African ethics to consider questions such as:

- Is there such a thing as a set of African ethics?
- What constitutes African ethics?
- Are African ethics consistent with, or different from, the prevailing set of Western ethics (however confusing and disarrayed Western ethics may seem to be)?
- Do African ethics have anything valuable to say, not only to an African context, but also in the wider world?

Subsequently, other scholars were invited to submit further chapters on specific issues related to African ethics and the book was shaped into its current form. It was agreed that if there is a set of African ethics that govern and guide the behaviour of African people, it is important to know what those guidelines are, otherwise we could try to impose upon the people of southern Africa a set of ethics drawn from elsewhere, probably from the colonial past, which do not sit well with African people. (For example, the growing criticism in some quarters of rulings of the Constitutional Court in South Africa on matters such as corporal punishment, same-sex marriages, or whether receiving gifts by ruling politicians amounts to corruption, or is merely part of African respect for those in authority, may stem from a clash between traditional African ethics and the human rights ethics derived basically from Western legal systems.) If there is a set of African ethics, are there things to be drawn from it that can usefully be applied in a wider context?

Although the focus in this book is on African ethics, we live, it is said, in a 'global village', meaning a world where national boundaries – cultural or geographical – have become blurred, a world in which a single economic system is emerging, where television and satellite telecommunications can (if programmers and watchers choose) bring world events wherever they occur to our homes at the moment that they happen. None of us remains unaffected by other cultures very different from our own. Muslim conservatism affects national security in the United States; commercialism in the United States affects Chinese farmers. The growth of industry in China and India means job losses in the United States and South Africa. In a world largely dominated by supposedly laissez-faire market forces, its economy dominated by global multinational companies, no part of the world is immune from gains or losses on the world stock markets – but equally no stock market is immune from minor palace revolutions in some small oil- or ore-producing country. Whether we like it or not, we are deeply affected by one another's fortunes and misfortunes. The days of people living in securely confined national or cultural compartments, if they ever existed, are over.

In this global environment, Africa is still perceived in many ways by the West as a 'dark continent': droughts, earthquakes and revolutions in Africa have little effect on world markets and for the most part, African culture remains opaque to the rest of the world. Africa is frequently seen as a place to be pitied, a continent of failure, which needs to be helped and guided by wiser, richer and more stable societies. Concerts such as Live 8 raise awareness of starving people in Africa and the G8 nations are urged to cancel the debt of African countries. Apart from wildlife sanctuaries and wilderness areas where foreign tourists may rediscover nature, Africa is seen to have little to contribute to the global village. It is consigned to the outskirts of the village; a beggar, an invalid, the 'sick man' of the modern world, just as the Ottoman Empire was seen as the 'sick man of Europe' at the start of the twentieth century. Yet, as was the case with Turkey in that period, the sickness is also seen as dangerous, a weak point in the construction of a global society, a source of infection and decay.

From an economic point of view, the world generally appears to think of Africa as backward and unproductive, or as a place to be exploited for its natural resources. Other nations, it is believed, need to manage and control those resources because Africans lack the technology or knowledge to do so. Much of the developed world expects Africa to be poor, inefficient and lacking in resourcefulness. Because it expects poor people to be ignorant and slow of understanding, there are few expectations that Africa will be able to manage its own affairs competently. This evokes an ambivalent response. On the one hand, the Western world is tempted to ignore Africa, to leave it to its fate, but on the other hand, it fears that the weaknesses and potential collapse of African society may cause collateral damage. Thus there is a feeling that the rest of the world should rush in and show African people better ways to manage their politics and their economies.

From an ethical point of view, Africa is regarded as an enigma. It evokes an ethical response from the world. Many people in richer countries are disturbed by pictures of starvation and put ethical pressure on their leaders to do something to help. However, they do not expect to learn any ethical lessons from Africa, except perhaps from the patient endurance of the poor. The developed world expects African countries to be beset by corruption. It expects African leaders to be mostly dishonest and concerned only for personal enrichment. Whether this is a fair assessment is another matter – if African leaders are bribable, it is often Western commercial enterprises that offer the bribes. It is unfair to regard Idi Amin, Jean-Bédel Bokassa, or Robert Mugabe as typical African leaders, rather than Julius Nyerere, Sir Seretse Khama or Nelson Mandela.

By contrast, however, and despite what is said above about the patronising attitude of much of the world towards Africa, there are signs in the field of ethics that Africa may be exercising considerable influence. Nelson Mandela has taken on the mantle of a modern secular saint and is one of the most well known international figures alive today. The South African Truth and Reconciliation Commission (TRC), although criticised in Chapter Four, is often taken as a model for the reconstruction of other broken societies. As far as religion is concerned, the majority of the world's Christians now live in Africa. The crisis in the Anglican Church over the ordination of an openly homosexual man as bishop in the United States and the reaction of the African dioceses has led to what is effectively a temporary exclusion of the United States Episcopalian Church from the worldwide Anglican Communion. The Archbishop of Nigeria and fellow African Anglican bishops seem to have forced the hand of the Archbishop of Canterbury and whatever the merits of the case, no one can doubt that African Christians have emerged as a major world voice.

It is the contention of the authors in this book that African views on ethics can make a major contribution towards an emerging global ethic. Several contributors point to the need for a global ethic. The culturally distinct ethics of separated cultures need to coalesce, so that we find some common core values. The word 'village' (as in 'global village') implies a community, which implies an agreement on the part of those living in the village to a set of behavioural principles that will protect and enhance community relationships and strictures on those behaviours that inhibit or damage community relationships. Some chapters in this book suggest (perhaps too optimistically) that there are already movements towards a global ethic that is wider than a Western one, incorporating principles drawn from Asia and the Islamic world, as well as from secular Western philosophy and Christian (or post-Christian) traditions. They suggest that Africa has an important contribution to make.

The need for a global ethic seems beyond doubt. In some ways talk of a global village is merely romantic. Although what we do in our separate cultural worlds affects those living in other worlds, we do not necessarily share common values, or even have much awareness of how what we do may affect others. Wars and the threat of wars still plague us and the fear of a nuclear attack has never disappeared, despite the end of the cold war. The poverty in many parts of the world is largely unabated. G8 nations, while recognising to a limited extent their obligation to alleviate poverty (even if only arguably for their own sakes) still cling to hugely protectionist measures designed to protect their wealth and to retain control of resources and capital. Conservative Islamic views clash tragically and violently with the values of a secular and mixed society. To some extent the same violent clash is seen when other religiously conservative groups object to those values – the bombing of abortion clinics is an example. Furthermore, far from consciously sharing a global ethic, our global village seems to be controlled by certain dominant cultures – at the moment, that of a capitalist and technological economy, but at times in the past, for parts of the world, the culture of Christendom, followed more recently by Marxist and collectivist worldviews. None of these granted much value to other worldviews, or to other concepts of right and wrong; all assumed that they were the whole and only truth.

It is against this background that some have begun grappling with formulating a global ethic, taking into account not only traditional Western secular and Christian views, but also those of other cultures, especially from Asia and elsewhere in the East. Yet in this discussion the voice of Africa remains largely unheard, perhaps because few people are aware that Africa has any contribution to make to the task. For example, in his important book on global ethics, Hans Küng, while considering the ethics of the religions of Europe and Asia, makes no reference to African ethics, despite the strong religious traditions of Africa (1998).

Several authors in this book suggest that traditional ethics of Africa need to be taken into account in any global ethic. Some suggest that this is so because otherwise Africans will be unmotivated and left out of the pervasive world of commerce and finance. Others (Augustine Shutte and Nhlanhla Mkhize) suggest that the traditional ethics of Africa have an important, even imperative, contribution to make to a global ethic and explore particularly the value of the traditional ethic of *ubuntu*. For example, in Chapter One, Shutte argues that the exponents of an African ethic 'must not simply rehearse its ancient wisdom in the forms in which it was first formulated', but must rearticulate its ethical insights to engage with other ethics and worldviews.

This is what this book sets out to do – to rearticulate African ethics, not simply on its own, but in dialogue with what contributors variously describe as the individualist, market-driven, predominantly Western values that inescapably dominate our world at present and, in subsequent chapters, to apply these ethics to specific issues such as gender, health, labour and economic issues.

Yet rearticulating African ethics is no easy task. To be sure, we can describe the ideas of *ubuntu* and *seriti*, of communal interdependence, of respect for ancestral wisdom, but to what extent these cultural values are still the values of Africa may be questioned. Despite, or, as some will argue in this book, even because of traditional values, Africa has huge ethical problems, which seem to call into question the idea that Africans live by *ubuntu*. Wars – over territory, ethnic and linguistic dominance and religion – still disfigure the continent. Some African leaders seem more concerned with personal enrichment and the ongoing control of power than with community welfare. This, of course, could be said of leaders anywhere, but in Africa, which is largely dependent on foreign aid and continually pleading for debt cancellation, the corruption of leaders and their civil servants seems particularly problematic. Aid given to ameliorate often ends up enriching the few.

Of course the fact that Africans do not always exemplify ideas such as *ubuntu* does not mean that traditional African values are discredited or of no significance, any more than the activities of some Middle Eastern rulers negate the validity of Islamic values, or the activities of President Bush and his advisers negate the validity of traditional Christian values. It is often true that people fail to live out their stated values. But the crises in Africa do mean that we must be careful not to overstate the hold that traditional African ethics have in practice in African society. They perhaps exist as a concept, as an ideal, as a lodestar, but not always as a fully lived reality.

There are also real problems in discerning whose ethics count as being African. Are we talking about the values derived from African traditional religion? Are the values derived from other religions present in Africa to be taken into account? Are we talking about values derived from the culture of those whose origins lie in Africa, and if so, do we include those of North Africa? What about other cultures now embedded in Africa – those of Arabia, or Europe?

Is there such a thing as African traditional religion as a unified entity, or are there simply myriads of traditional African religions? The consensus of scholars is that although traditional religion takes on subtly different forms in different parts of Africa, there are nevertheless overriding universal features, which allow us to talk of a single African traditional religion, rather than a number of different religions. Contributors to this book take different stances on the role of religion in Africa. Some assume and even state explicitly that all ethics in Africa are derived from a religious outlook. Others argue that while religious beliefs of various kinds are widespread, traditional African ethics override and transcend the perceived supernatural origins of ethics and are universal in Africa despite religious differences, or the absence of religious belief and the onset of secularisation.

Tradition does not remain static. Although no doubt still influenced by earlier traditional beliefs and practices, most Africans are Christians or Muslims of one sort or another. By using the term, 'African ethics', are we excluding Christian and Muslim ethics? Have not traditional beliefs already been inextricably influenced by these evangelising world faiths, as well as by the ubiquitous presence of Western commercialism? By 'African ethics', do we mean only the ethics of those whose origins lie in Africa, or do we include the ethics of those living in Africa whose origins lie in Europe, or the Asian subcontinent, or Indonesia? Should we include the ethics of the Muslim states north of the Sahara? Especially in South Africa, where although the majority of persons are of African origin, there are those whose ancestral origins lie in Europe or Asia, but whose recent ancestors have lived in Africa over several generations, and where there is also a large population of persons with mixed ethnic ancestry, are they and their ethical outlooks to be regarded as African? These are sensitive issues.

'African ethics' could arguably include the ethics of everybody who lives in Africa. Some of these people, even those whose ancestral origins lie in Africa, will be Christian or Muslim, but their Christian or Islamic beliefs will have been influenced and shaped by their earlier traditions. Because of the huge influence of Christianity and Islam in Africa it would be intolerably narrow to restrict the meaning of African ethics so as to exclude them. However, the ethics of Christian or Muslim Africans may well be somewhat different in emphasis to those of Christians in the West or Muslims in Arabia and Asia.

In this book, to keep our canvas manageable, the ethics that we are talking about are the ethics of people whose outlook and roots of origin lie in sub-Saharan Africa and predominantly in southern Africa, but are also inevitably in dialogue with Christian ethics and the ethics of global capitalism, both of which are so influential in southern Africa.

There is, however, a gap in the book. Amongst the earliest inhabitants of southern Africa are the people now described as the Khoi and the San.

The former were mostly pastoralists and have been largely absorbed now into the rest of the southern African population. Their history is an oral history and we have no written access to their thoughts. No doubt their views on interpersonal relationships and between people and the world of nature have also been absorbed in to what we now call African ethics. The San still exist as a distinct population group, although in small numbers and increasingly mixed with other groups. They were mostly nomadic and thanks to the work of people such as Wilhelm Bleek and Lucy Lloyd, who first captured their stories in print, as well as the legacy of their rock engravings and rock paintings, we have some idea of their thoughts, conjectural though our ideas may be (see Hollmann 2004). They lived (and in a few cases live still) in small family groups far removed from the modern global society with which this book seeks to engage. Yet it seems clear that the San have much to teach us, especially about the interdependence of humans and animals and perhaps a modern spokesperson from within those owing their heritage to the San needs to be found who can add that voice to what we mean by African ethics. At present, however, it must be admitted that those writing about African ethics rarely, if ever, refer to the San.

As well as being descriptive of African ethics, the authors of this book feel that it is important to subject traditional African ethics to a critique. As we have already asked, is the notion of *ubuntu* really a description of African society? Can *ubuntu* work beyond small communities and be applied when the community in question is a heterogeneous, large city, or nation, or global community, where many faiths coexist? In a rapidly changing world and as African states seek to find a place in a competitive global environment, are traditional values still relevant? Are some aspects of traditional African culture – male hegemony, respect for elders and chiefs, the idea that a fortunate individual must share his or her fortune with the wider family in assisting them with jobs – not tantamount to sexism, gerontocracy, authoritarianism, nepotism, and the like? Should we still take seriously the African idea that illness and misfortune are due to ancestral displeasure; should modern hospitals find a place for *umuthi* and the ministrations of the *isangoma*?

Several contributors to this book comment on the notion of *seriti*, a quality that is complementary to *ubuntu*. *Seriti* is a quality of power that is invested in a person. It is the respect with which a person is regarded in the community. A person may gain *seriti* by undergoing religious rituals or rites of passage. A person may have *seriti* by virtue of his/her position of leadership in society and by virtue of his/her qualities of oratory, persuasiveness and power to influence others. But for our purposes in this book, we note that *seriti* also means the quality that is reflected through a person's good works and wisdom. Anyone who contributes to wholeness and equilibrium has *seriti*, i.e has earned respect in the community and that respect is prized above worldly wealth, positions, or status. It does a person no good to have many possessions, but no respect from the community. Private and unshared wealth does not bring *seriti*. Thus, a person who has gained wealth, or who has the power to distribute favours will seek to share that wealth in order to gain respect. This begs the question: does this concept feed into the ongoing scandals in our society to do with jobs for friends, or nepotism?

There is much emphasis in African ethics in values being communal rather than individualistic, on decisions being made not by fiat, or even by majority vote, but by consensus. The emphasis on communal values means that in African tradition, community decisions are by preference made by consensus rather than by an individual – although the elders and those who by their ordered life have commanded respect or *seriti*, have a particular contribution to make. What perhaps needs more examination is the extent to which the emphasis on consensus makes decision-making slow and cumbersome in a world where often quick decisions need to be made to stay in control, but also the extent to which the emphasis on consensus means that decisions will often be too conservative, too closed to necessary change and too disadvantageous to the weak and voiceless in the community, particularly to women.

In defence of *ubuntu* we must reiterate the point; *ubuntu* is concerned with the welfare of everyone in the community. In theory, at least, it is intended to ensure that no voice goes unheard. Although the welfare of the community is the basis of the welfare of individuals, the welfare of the community depends upon individuals being cared for. Where the needs of individuals – especially powerless individuals – are ignored or overridden, the peace and equilibrium of the community are thereby harmed. Thus a necessary balance has to be maintained. Yet because it is so easy for consensus to mean in practice that the voice of the powerful elders prevails, the emphasis on individual rights that is so typical of Western human rights documents has its place (see Mutombo 2007 for a discussion on the difference between African human rights and those of the Universal Declaration of Human Rights). Nevertheless, in attempting to create a shared global ethic, it seems that the concept of *ubuntu*, with its emphasis on listening to all views, seeking a consensus based on respect for all and the creation of a stable, harmonious and balanced state of equilibrium has much to offer.

The first two contributors, Mkhize and Shutte, lay the foundations on which the book is based. In Chapter One, Shutte compares *ubuntu* with classical Western philosophy. He reiterates what this Introduction has identified as a need for a global ethic in a global society, a need for a 'common language' in ethics. He affirms that the dominant culture and value system in the world at present, however flawed, is a technological and monetarist value system originating in Europe. Thus, we cannot escape from this dominant culture, but we can engage with it critically. In his view, there are important themes in traditional African ethics that both question and complement the dominant European culture. With this in mind, he provides an historical overview of European ethics, from the Greeks to the present, but with a particular emphasis on some themes drawn from Thomas Aquinas by modern Thomists, in particular the ideas of 'intersubjectivity' and 'self-realization'. He then draws our attention to similarities between these concepts and those of *ubuntu* and *seriti*.

In Chapter Two, Mkhize points to the centrality of the well-known concept of *ubuntu* as a basis for African ethics. *Ubuntu* is not only concerned with relationships between people, but is the basis of relationships between people and God, people and their ancestors, people and the rest of the created world. Mkhize places the notion of *ubuntu* firmly within a religious worldview (which other contributors to the book might question). He suggests that *ubuntu* is closely parallel to the ancient Egyptian concept of Maat and thus has a long and respected African heritage. He provides a philosophical and theological basis for *ubuntu*, quoting notable African scholars to support his thesis and shows the African stress on harmony, balance and a complementary hierarchy of being. He indicates the importance and place of the ancestors in this communitarian worldview of the self and of society and points out that an African view of human rights differs somewhat from the individualistic emphases of the Universal Bill of Rights.

Having set the scene, the following chapters each take one issue in modern life, especially in South Africa, and examine how traditional African ethics might engage with this issue. One of the crucial issues facing sub-Saharan Africa is that of HIV and AIDS. The question has to be asked: if Africa has embraced Christian and Islamic values including those concerning sexual behaviour, or if traditional African values place such emphasis on community well-being, how can it be that the virus has taken such hold in sub-Saharan Africa? In Chapter Three, Ezra Chitando suggests that it is in part because neither religious nor traditional values adequately challenge the hegemonic masculinity so common in Africa. Chitando is not suggesting that in other societies men are less dominating, but that the idea of male supremacy is a major factor in the spread of HIV. Thus, he is suggesting that in fact African values, whether Christian or traditional, need to be challenged and changed. There are, he suggests, subtexts in these worldviews that do allow for the protection of women and these subtexts need to be made more dominant. Chitando is pointing to the need for African ethics (whether Christian or traditional) to be constantly revised and fine-tuned to meet new issues. We should not be merely looking to the past to see what values have been held historically, but also see African ethics as a dynamic and self-modifying process.

While many believe that the TRC in South Africa was a major factor in allowing the country to transform without civil war, in Chapter Four, R. Neville Richardson traces the thoughts of several scholars of African philosophy and ethics who believe that the TRC ignored African values in favour of a particular set of liberal individualist values and that therefore far from creating true reconciliation, it has left many feeling bitter and unheard. He quotes Wim van Binsbergen who alleges that the oppressed majority in South Africa were further oppressed when the very terms of reconciliation that they were expected to embrace were dictated by Western Christian values. Although Archbishop Tutu, the chairperson of the TRC, frequently referred to *ubuntu* as a guiding principle, Richardson shows Van Binsbergen's belief that Tutu's understanding of *ubuntu* is a skewed and Christianised version.

In Chapter Five, Munyaradzi Felix Murove tackles the issue of capitalism and whether the more communal emphasis in African ethics might provide a better basis for commerce and business in Africa. He notes that business studies in South Africa are heavily biased towards a neo-liberal form of capitalism. He points to the problems that global capitalism has caused in Africa, especially because the form of capitalism that reached colonial Africa was a debased form of capitalism. Quoting Ali Mazrui, he suggests that capitalism in Africa has meant the acquisition of wealth without the accompanying work or frugality associated with the 'Protestant work ethic'. Instead, the Africans worked, while the white overseer took his ease. He posits alternative and more African foundations for business, such as *ujamaa* and *harambee*. At the same time, he admits that if Africa is to be economically competitive, it is important that the energy, efficiency and edge that neo-liberal capitalism arguably creates should not be lost.

In much the same way, in Chapter Six, John Mtyuwafhethu Mafunisa examines labour issues and the motivation of the work force in the light of African ethics. He suggests that the labour force, predominantly African, is in fact still hugely influenced by traditional perspectives and therefore any attempt to motivate them to work harder or to be more honest that is not framed in terms of an ethic that is familiar to them is bound to fail.

Finally, Lucinda Domoko Manda suggests in Chapter Seven that a more holistic view of healing, such as is found in a traditional African approach, which includes relational and spiritual issues, as well as medicinal and what might be regarded as the predominantly physical emphases of Western healing, are not only more appealing to African people, fitting with their world of meaning, but may also offer complementary emphases for Western medicine.

In short, then, our quest is to understand what ethical values hold sway in our African context. By what values do African people actually live? Where do these values come from? Do they work? Are they appropriate, given the issues that face us? In what way do they need modifying or complementing? Those of us from a Western background want to know what we can learn from an African worldview. Those of us whose background is African may also need to learn from and borrow from values from elsewhere as we face new and uncharted waters. Nothing remains static and unchanging.

Thus the task of the African Ethics Initiative that this book tentatively begins, is in part historical (what were the values of the past?), in part anthropological (what are the current values in African culture?), in part comparative (how do the ethics of Africa fit with or differ from other ethical traditions?) and in large part, creative and persuasive (what ought our ethical values to be given the needs of our context?).

Although our canvas is Africa, especially sub-Saharan Africa, our special interest is in southern Africa, where in many ways African and other cultures are more roughly thrown together and where perhaps, because colonialism lasted for so much longer, the voice of Africa has been more silent and dishonoured.

If the global village needs a global ethic to live by, South Africa, rainbow nation or not, is equally in desperate need of an ethic to which all can give allegiance. We still face huge inequalities of wealth and unacceptable levels of poverty for many of our people. Corruption and white-collar crime seem to be endemic in the political and business worlds. Robbery, rape, murder and all kinds of violent crime make the lives of many, but especially the lives of the poor, unendurable. The abuse of women and children gives constant concern and the prevalence of HIV and AIDS suggests that our sexual mores need urgent attention.

If an ethic is to be widely accepted, it needs to mesh with what people really believe in their hearts, but because we come from different backgrounds, our beliefs may be widely disparate. Especially since most of our people come from African roots, a communal ethic needs to mesh with what Africans really believe; yet we need to search for commonalities so that others of European or Asian backgrounds can also buy into the ethic. This is the challenge that faces us if our society is to be one in which all are glad to play their part.

Select bibliography

Hollmann, Jeremy C. (ed.). 2004. *Customs and Beliefs of the !Xam Bushmen*. Johannesburg: University of Witwatersrand Press.

Küng, Hans. 1998. *A Global Ethic for Global Politics and Economics*. Oxford: Oxford University Press.

Mutombo, Nkulu. 'The African Charter on Human and People's Rights: An African Contribution to the Project of Global Ethics'. http://astro.temple.edu/~dialogue/Center/mutombo.htm (accessed 30 October 2007).

1

African Ethics in a Globalising World

AUGUSTINE SHUTTE

THE WORLD OF the twenty-first century is a globalising one. Connections and communications between human beings increasingly cover and surround the earth. There is a huge variety of them: telephone systems, television networks, e-mail, the Internet, air and shipping lines, multinational companies, economic and political associations. These all have a certain unifying effect; they put us in touch with one another. But they also reveal the diversity of the world; we are constantly faced with difference – of geography, lifestyle, culture and religion. This interplay of unity and diversity is the defining feature of our age. It shows itself in the most dramatic way in the difference of resources between the developed and under-developed parts of the world, the First World and the Third, North and South, and the way in which these different regions are locked together by economic and political forces.

This imbalance of resources is only the most striking example of a human problem that is also a global one. There are others: the destruction of the environment, AIDS, terrorism and fundamentalism. Increasingly human problems such as these affect everyone. However, responses to them are very different and it is increasingly difficult to find a basis for agreement between all those who are affected. For this reason, we live in under constant threat of violence, a state of permanent cold war.

In an attempt to find a solution to this problem, the Parliament of the World's Religions, as well as other world organisations, has launched a project to produce a 'global ethic', a set of ethical values to which everyone – however different their traditions and cultures – could subscribe to. This project is well under way and seems to be achieving something of substance. But, perhaps understandably, it is dominated by voices from the United States and Europe. More recently Eastern and Asiatic influences have been included. African voices, however, have not. Perhaps this is because Africa is seen as a disaster area, the place where all the problems I have mentioned are most in evidence, a sort of ethical black hole. Perhaps, however, it is because Africa is not seen as having anything special to offer, any ethical insights of its own. And this is a serious mistake that those of us who live and work here must try to overcome. However difficult the notion of Africa or African is to define, there can be no doubt that there exists a characteristic indigenous ethical tradition or set of traditions in sub-Saharan Africa that has certain common characteristics. What is more important is the fact that this embodies ethical insights that are both true and important in themselves, and are also significantly lacking in the dominant ethical thinking in the global community.

There is no doubt that the dominant global culture is European, in the sense that it is a culture formed by the science and technology (and the industrialisation and capitalism) that originated in Europe in the seventeenth and eighteenth centuries and, of course, this culture has its own ethical traditions. No culture and hence no ethical tradition, is immune from ethical criticism and there is every indication that the dominant scientific technological culture is ethically impoverished. There seems to be no way to find an objective universal ethic.

There is no avoiding an engagement with European culture and European ethics in our contemporary globalising world and if it is a critical engagement, so much the better. If Africa is to play a part in the worldwide ethical discussion, it cannot be content simply to rehearse its ancient wisdom in the forms in which it was first formulated. It has to find a way of articulating its ethical insights that can engage with a scientific culture. South Africa provides an ideal setting for developing this ethical dialogue between Africa and Europe. Two features especially make this country unique in Africa. The first is the fact that it is the one colonial country where Europeans have stayed and it is the most developed country in Africa, First World and Third World in one place. The second feature is apartheid. More than in any other country in Africa, Europeans and Africans in South Africa were separated from each other. Now, since the ending of apartheid and the beginning of our programme of nation-building, we are, as a consequence, more aware of and engaged with the issues of identity and diversity than anywhere else. Our Truth and Reconciliation Commission was only the initiation of a process that still continues.

From this position I want to suggest a point of contact between the two ethical traditions, African and European, and to offer my own contribution to the formulation of a common language in which to express what I believe is a complementary wisdom. I write as a 'European' South African, whose European culture has been acquired in an African context, and for this reason has an African connection. The bulk of this chapter will take the form of a historical sketch of the European ethical tradition in order to identify what I take to be the enduring insights that it embodies. I will then try to show how these can be connected to certain key insights in the African tradition. By European ethics, I mean the ethics that European culture has produced and carried with it wherever it has gone – initially to the United States and the various European colonies, but by now to virtually the whole world. I do this in order to distinguish this philosophical tradition from the forms of thought, worldviews and systems of values of the cultures at present being obliterated by this growth. In particular I wish to distinguish it from certain traditional African ideas concerning the nature of persons and morality that seem to me to be remarkably consonant with at least one kind of contemporary European philosophy.

The historical roots

The tradition of European ethics has two main roots, a Greek root and a biblical root. The Greek root is the idea of *physis*, nature. To act morally is to act in conformity with our nature. Human nature is defined by genus and species: we are members of the animal genus and our specific difference is reason – we are rational animals. So to live in accordance with our nature is to live in accordance with reason. The fulfillment of our nature (which alone can make us truly happy) consists in the exercise of our highest power, the mind, in contemplation, together with the integration of all our powers, cognitive, volitional and emotional, by the wisdom such contemplation can achieve.

Such harmonious development of our powers is what is known as virtue. In addition to the highest virtue of wisdom, there are the four cardinal virtues of prudence, justice, courage and self-control. Wisdom consists in the knowledge of the ultimate goals of human life, prudence in the ability to discern ways of achieving them. Justice regulates and orders the actions and social practices whereby we try to put this understanding into effect. On the one hand, courage and self-control are the emotions that enable us to overcome difficulties and threats to our success in this endeavour, and on the other hand, they lead us to love and desire that which our reason reveals as truly desirable and lovable.

The Greek concept of morality is that it is concerned with perfecting our human nature so that we are able to live happily in the harmonious exercise of all our powers. There is an analogy here with physical health. Medical treatment is concerned with our physical health, morality with our psychic health. The context in which the moral life is lived is the small self-governing city-state. Social harmony is necessary for a happy life, but it is only possible if the individuals who make up the state and govern it have themselves achieved an inner integration through the cultivation of the virtues.

The biblical root of the European ethical tradition is very different. The setting that gives the moral life its point and purpose is poles apart from the peaceful order of the small Greek city-state. The biblical idea is based on a project to build a city in which the whole of humanity can find a home, and a people to which the whole of humanity will belong. The life of this city, this people, will be a life that transcends every limitation including death. This is because, according to the biblical vision, humanity is 'the image of God' and so, like God, in some way transcendent. For this reason, human life and history can only be brought to fulfillment by a transcendent power, the power of the creator. So the city will be the city of God and the people will be the people of God. God will make his home there and be its ruler.

The Bible documents the struggle to bring such a kingdom of God into being. Human history is understood as the struggle between humanity (represented by the people of Israel) and God (represented by the prophets and eventually, Jesus) to realise this aim. There is a continuing war between the human power of sin and God's power of grace. Humanity seeks to build the city through asserting its own finite powers, seeking a limitless good in its own limited creation. This idolatry divides both the human heart and the human community, producing both inner and outer conflict and oppression. God, on the other hand, persists with his plan to make humanity his holy people. He reveals his character and the character of the eternal life that we are to share with him by means of his word, in the commandments of the Old Testament and then in Jesus in the New. He empowers us to live this life by means of his own spirit that he puts into our hearts. This then is the dramatic setting of the biblical understanding of morality.

The whole point of morality is to express in human life the character of God and his eternal life. This is revealed in the Old Testament, especially in the Ten Commandments. So the key concept here is that of law, understood as the form of a communication from God to humanity and expressive of his will. This is of the utmost importance: the biblical concept of law, and of morality as obedience to law, derives from the idea of a personal transaction between God and humanity, a transaction initiated by God and involving both promises and commands. There is thus nothing impersonal about the notion. As the prophet Jeremiah has God say, 'I will put my law within them, and I will write it upon their hearts; and I will be their God, and they shall be my people' (Jer. 31:31). Even in the New Testament, the idea of law is used to refer to the most intimate personal contact between God and humanity, the exchange in which grace produces faith. As Thomas Aquinas puts it: 'The new law primarily consists of the grace of the Holy Spirit showing itself in faith working through love' (*Summa Theologiae*, 1a2ae.106, 1).

The medieval synthesis: The idea of natural law

Nature and law thus identify the two roots of the European tradition of philosophical ethics. They grow together in the theology of the church, and weave and interweave throughout the Middle Ages. Finally, in the thirteenth century, the definitive synthesis of Greek and biblical thought is achieved in the thought of Thomas Aquinas. Part of this synthesis is the connecting of the ideas of nature and law in the concept of natural law.

The basis for this synthesis is the belief that it is one and the same God who reveals his will for us in the Commandments (the old law) in the Old Testament and the moral teaching of Jesus (the new law) in the New, and who, as our creator, is the author of our human nature with its rational capacity for self-knowledge and self-determination. Thus, in principle, there is no conflict between what faith tells us and what we can know by the use of our reason, between what God has commanded and the deep desires of a nature created in his image.

In the idea of natural law, Aquinas presents us with a conception of morality as living according to the God-given tendencies of our human nature, so as to obey his command to realise ourselves in his image, so that we become capable of sharing his eternal life, which transcends both sin and death. The worldview of Christian faith has replaced Greek philosophy as the context for the development of our natural powers towards their fulfillment. Although this is not enough to fit us for this transcendent life, it is necessary. Nature is made for grace; as Aquinas would say, grace does not ignore nature, but perfects it.

From a philosophical point of view, this idea of natural law is important, since, in principle, it is knowable by reason. Thus according to Aquinas, we are able to identify the basic tendencies, the natural desires, of our nature. These form an integrated system whose foundation is the desire to realise our specifically human capacities, such as those for knowledge, for love, for creativity, for play, for worship and so on. Because all human beings share the same human nature, the idea of natural law provides an objective foundation for morality that is not relative to a particular society, culture or period.

The modern development: The separation of law and nature

The history of European ethics after Aquinas is one of progressive separation of the two elements contained in the idea of natural law, namely law and nature. There were numerous causes of this split, but the most important was the development of the natural sciences in the modern period.

Modern science produced a quite different attitude to and idea of nature. Scientific method comprised two elements: observation and measurement. Nature as the object studied by science was therefore understood as what was observable and measurable. And knowing it in this way enabled us to control it; this was the ultimate vindication of scientific method. It did not take long before this conception of nature was applied to human nature as well.

In a scientific context, the idea of law also underwent a similar transformation. The laws of nature that science dealt with were not in any sense commands, telling us how we *ought* to behave; they were merely the expression of general regularities that explained how things actually *did* behave. They had therefore no moral force at all. There is no connection between the truths science discovers about our human nature and the goals we ought to strive for in order to be good, no way of deriving an *ought* from an *is*.

Philosophy during the modern period developed on two different lines: empiricism and rationalism. Each line emphasised one of the elements that were combined in scientific method. Empiricism emphasised the element of observation and experiment. The foundation of knowledge was sense experience and the object of knowledge was a sensible nature. Knowledge was understood as a kind of seeing, seeing things as they really were, and what they were was material bodies. Empiricism and materialism were intrinsically connected. Rationalism emphasised the role of reason in science, reason being understood narrowly and abstractly, as a power of organisation and calculation, rather than as insight into reality.

In an empiricist climate of thought, morality was also understood as a matter of sensation, but internal rather than external sensation. This line of philosophical ethics found its classical expression in the work of Hume, for whom moral judgements were the expression of particular feelings of pleasure or pain produced by the observation of people's behaviour. In Hume's view, what we find pleasant or painful is determined by the human nature we all have in common. Hence moral judgements for Hume were descriptive of certain general truths about what would make us happy or unhappy. The purpose of morality was to produce the greatest preponderance of pleasurable over painful feelings. Hume's approach to morality is the ancestor of the utilitarian approach to ethics in contemporary European philosophy.

In a rationalist climate of thought, morality was understood as a system of laws derivable from some fundamental self-evident principle, rather as the theorems of geometry are derivable from fundamental axioms. To act morally was to act in accordance with rational laws, which, since they were all derived from the same principle, would be the same for all. The classical statement of this idea of morality was Kant's. To be moral was to be rational, not in the Greek or medieval sense of acting according to one's rational nature, but in the sense of acting according to the abstract idea of rationality, the pure idea of law itself. Action according to the pure idea of law was the only genuine moral action, or, to put it more simply, doing one's duty for duty's sake. Kant had a great influence on European ethics, which lives on today in all forms of duty-ethics (often called deontological) and in the idea of moral *rights*.

The separation of the ideas of nature and law in relation to morality in the modern period has resulted in the two main contemporary forms of European ethics: the utilitarian and the deontological. Utilitarianism is consequentialist, in that it ties morality to the consequences of our acts, whether they produce more pleasure than pain. Deontological ethics is, as the name implies, concerned with the principle on which we act; is the principle of our action capable of being universalised in a law-like way?

Each of these approaches to morality embodies something that should be regarded as central to morality. Utilitarianism is concerned that the consequences of our acts should contribute to human welfare, such welfare being determined by some reference to natural feelings of pleasure and pain. Deontological ethics is concerned with the normative and overriding force of morality and seeks to secure this by connecting morality to rationality. Each however, by emphasising one central aspect in isolation from the other, distorts morality. Human nature is not, as utilitarianism implies, merely an object the sciences are able to investigate. Nor is reason, as the idea of duty for duty's sake implies, an abstract system of principles separate from our concrete human nature. The source of both errors is the scientific idea of nature that comes eventually to be applied to human nature too.

European philosophy in the modern period (roughly from the end of the fifteenth to the beginning of the nineteenth century) is characterised by a huge forgetfulness of the human person. The philosophers of the period are so hypnotised by science (and also by the technology that science made possible), so extroverted into the observable and measurable world, that they quite forget themselves as people. This is not just a matter of focusing on the world of nature, rather than on human beings. This forgetfulness of the human person continues even after the rise of the human sciences, as opposed to the natural sciences, such as history, sociology or psychology. In fact, it is here that it becomes more clearly apparent – and more dangerous.

Modern European philosophy overlooks the fact that people are subjects as well as objects. As knowing subjects, human beings are the producers, the *creators* of science; as acting subjects, we are the agents who change the world by technology and work. Science however (not only the human sciences) studies us (and technology increasingly manipulates us) as objects. In so doing, it misses the most important aspect of human nature, the fact that we are knowing and acting subjects. It is precisely our ability to think and choose that makes us moral beings. Forgetfulness of this aspect of our human nature makes it impossible either to relate morality to human nature, or to give an adequate account of morality.

It is as subjects that human beings are the originators of both science and moral action in the world. Ironically it is precisely in the modern period that our subjectivity is most fully displayed, in our growing understanding and control of our environment. It is these developments that make possible an insight into human nature that was not possible before. As psychologically acute as Aquinas is, he still approaches human nature within a broadly cosmological vision of the world, as occupying a particular place in the hierarchy of being, as one species among others.

The discovery of human subjectivity has enabled contemporary Thomist philosophers such as Lonergan, Rahner, McIntyre, McCabe, Meynell and others to reconnect morality with human nature in a renewal of Aquinas' theory of natural law. Such a development is at odds with the dominant forms of contemporary European ethics, both in its materialist (or dualist) understanding of human nature that derives from a connection with the sciences, and in its utilitarian (or deontological) conception of ethics. It is however far more open than other kinds of European philosophy to non-European forms of thought. In particular, the conception of human beings on which this new form of ethical thinking is based, exhibits a striking consonance with certain ideas about human nature that are central to traditional African ethics.

The emergence of an awareness of human subjectivity begins as far back as Kant in the European philosophical tradition. However, in Kant, it is expressed in strongly dualistic terms. The rational subject of thought and action (and hence of morality) is sharply separated from the phenomenal self that is part of nature and history. Hegel sought to close this gap, making humanity the ultimate product and the subject of nature and history. In the process, however, he appears to reduce reality to ideas, history to the development of a single universal spirit.

It is only with Kierkegaard and the development of the existentialist and phenomenological movements in European philosophy, that human subjectivity begins to be explored in a thorough and concrete way. At the same time, the human sciences, especially the social sciences, begin to provide varied insights into environmental influences on people and the causal links that connect them to impersonal nature. In spite of growing insight into the links between human subjects and the natural and social worlds, modern science operates within a radically materialist framework.

During the modern period, the philosophical tradition centred on Aquinas went underground, being kept alive chiefly by the Catholic Church, in which it had been canonised as the 'perennial philosophy'. As such, it was simplified and vulgarised and reduced to a form that could be easily assimilated by those training to be priests. In the twentieth century, however, a resurrection of authentic Thomist philosophy took place, begun by philosophers and historians of philosophy such as Jacques Maritain and Etienne Gilson, but then continued in a creative way by thinkers such as Rahner and Lonergan.

Aquinas had inherited the Aristotelian conception of human nature, in which soul and body were related as form and matter in the one human individual. Aquinas understood this in a way that avoided both the body-soul dualism of Plato and the materialism of the pre-Socratics. Nevertheless the language he had inherited from the Greek philosophers was always open to misunderstanding in a dualistic way, especially in the modern period, where the only alternative to materialism was understood to be substantial body-soul dualism of a Cartesian kind.

Reformulating Aquinas
Contemporary Thomists such as Rahner, who have learnt from existential and phenomenological philosophy, as well as from the human sciences, have reformulated Aquinas' understanding of human nature in a way that makes our subjectivity central, while at the same time avoiding any form of dualism.

The subjectivity of people is our capacity to originate thought and action. As such, we are both self-conscious and self-determining. In human self-consciousness, the self is both the one who knows and the one who is known, both subject and object at once. The same is true of human self-determination; we are both the subject who acts and the object who is acted upon. We bring ourselves to act. As subjects, human beings are self-enacting, self-realising. As such, we transcend the influences of all external causes whatsoever; we are free. This is not to say that the causes that science discovers, whether social or natural, cease to operate within us; it would be absurd to say so. They are necessary, but not sufficient to explain what we think and do.

As subjects, human beings are constituted by this twofold internal relationship to themselves, through which we both know ourselves and affirm ourselves as self-realising. But this is not all we are. We also exist in relationship to what is other than ourselves, to our natural and social environment and, especially, to other people. This is the relationship that is studied in so many varied ways by the sciences.

Taken together, the sciences reveal the forms of our dependence on what is other than ourselves for our existence and our characters. Such dependence is radical; without it, we cannot think or act, be self-consciousness or self-determining. Without a sensible environment, we can have no sensations; without sensations, no images; without images, no thoughts. Without thoughts, there can be no self-awareness. And similarly, without feelings, we can have no emotions; without emotions, we cannot choose; without choices, we cannot act. No action means no self-realisation. We are dependent on what is other than ourselves for our self-consciousness and self-determination. Such dependence is not sufficient to make us self-enacting, self-realising beings, but it is necessary.

This necessity is especially evident in our relationship to other people. In addition to the variety of ways in which our dependence on our social and natural environment is revealed by the different sciences, there is a unique form of dependence on other persons for the exercise, development and fulfillment of precisely that capacity that makes us persons and subjects, the capacity for self-awareness and self-determination. It is especially this unique intersubjective relationship between persons, and the forms it takes in human life and growth, which has been the centre of interest for contemporary Thomist philosophers influenced by existential and phenomenological philosophy. There is not space here to give a detailed picture of the account of intersubjectivity given by Thomist philosophers such as Donceel (1967), Johann (1966, 1975, 1976), Luijpen (1960), Nedoncelle (1966), Toner (1968) and others. Here I want to stress just one aspect of intersubjectivity that this body of work reveals.

It is an important, although paradoxical, feature of the dependence of human beings on other people for their development as persons that it is precisely through this dependence that their capacity for self-determination is developed. Self-determination and dependence on others appear to be strict alternatives. And so they are, in relationships between impersonal realities and also in those social relationships that are not properly intersubjective. The more that one is influenced by another, the less self-determining one is. However, when a relationship between people is consciously and deliberately enacted, a relationship thus of subject to subject, quite the opposite is the case. The more I am influenced by the other, the more an act is my own and the more self-determining I become.

One can get an idea of this paradoxical growth of freedom-in-dependence by considering examples where it does not occur. A good example is that of so-called 'wild children', children who have grown to physical maturity away from any contact with other people. In the few cases where careful study has been possible, it is apparent that these children have failed to develop as people, as responsible subjects of thought and action. Something similar is found in cases of 'hospitalism', where babies have grown up in institutions without the normal personal attention from a caring parent. They were in contact with nurses, but due to the number of babies to each nurse, relationships between nurse and baby could only be functional and not properly personal.

The Thomist authors referred to earlier present extremely rich analyses of the various forms taken by the intersubjective transaction between persons that brings about the development of our capacity for self-realisation. What emerges from this body of work is that it is only in certain kinds of relationship with other persons that this capacity is developed, those in which one is known and affirmed as the person one is by one who both knows and is able to affirm themselves. The reasons for this are too lengthy to go into here, but there are two features of this account of the necessary conditions for personal growth that are relevant to our interests in this chapter.

The first is the reciprocity involved in the interpersonal transaction productive of personal growth. In order to develop as a person, I need to be known and affirmed by one who has self-knowledge and the ability to affirm themselves. Their affirmation of me enables me to come to know and affirm them. And this brings about a fuller knowledge and affirmation of myself. As the transaction proceeds, it is always the case that the more I know and affirm the other for their own sake, the more I become able to know and affirm myself. The more I am able to know and affirm myself, the more I will naturally come to know and affirm others for their own sake too.

Secondly, if it is true that a certain kind of dependence on other people is necessary for me to develop as a person, namely as a free, self-determining subject, then we have discovered a way of understanding human beings that does justice to their subjectivity, and so is not materialist, but is not dualistic either. As subjects, people are self-determining and hence transcend the influence of the kind of causes the sciences can discover. As human subjects, however, we depend on the influence, the strictly personal causality, of other persons for the exercise and growth of this capacity for self-realisation towards fulfillment.

Traditional African thought

We have thus arrived at a conception of human nature that does justice to our subjectivity, our ability to be the originators of thought and action, and hence should be able to provide a foundation for ethics as well. Before showing how this can be done, I want to bring out the connection between this conception of human nature and two ideas that are central to a traditional African understanding of people. These are the ideas, expressed in Zulu and Sotho, of *umuntu ngumuntu ngabantu* and *seriti*. The first expression, which can be translated to mean that a person is a person through other people, presents us with the distinctive idea of community that underlies so much of African culture, traditional practices and institutions. It is a view of community that is sharply opposed to all kinds of individualism. It is, however, equally opposed to collectivism of a European kind.

Menkiti distinguishes the African idea of community from 'an aggregated sum of individuals'. African thought, he says, 'asserts an ontological independence to human society, and moves from society to individuals', rather than, in the manner of European thought, 'from individuals to society' (1979, 165–67). Likewise, Senghor distinguishes the African view of community from the best-known European ones, all of which he labels as 'collectivist', in a negative sense. He is especially concerned to differentiate the African view from any form of communism or European socialism, speaking instead of a 'community society' and coining the term 'communalism' to express the African conception. It is, he holds, 'a community-based society, communal, not collectivist. We are concerned here, not with a mere collection of individuals, but with people conspiring together, *con-spiring* in the basic Latin sense, united among themselves even to the very centre of their being' (1963, 16).

The reason that Senghor is so concerned to distinguish the African view of community from all forms of European collectivism is his belief that the latter undermine the dignity and value of individual persons. He speaks of traditional African society being 'based both on the community and on the person and in which, because it was founded on dialogue and reciprocity, the group had priority over the individual without crushing him [or her], but allowing him [or her] to blossom as a person' (1966, 5).

It is useful to see dialogue or conversation as the typical activity and, indeed, the ultimate purpose of a community as understood in traditional African thought, since this is a co-operative activity that is achieved simply by the presence of people, rather than by them fulfilling any further function, as would be the case in some practical activity such as building a house.

Perhaps the best model for community as understood in African thought is the family. The family has no function outside itself. It is a means of personal growth for its members, and the interaction, the conversation and companionship between the growing and fully-grown members is also an end in itself. African culture is famous for its notion of the extended family (now seriously threatened by the advancing tide of European culture in its present form). The extended family is capable of extension to include anyone, not only those related by blood, kinship or marriage. In the last resort, humanity itself is conceived of as a family, a family that one joins at birth, but does not leave by dying. Because of this, no one is a stranger. The world is our common home and the earth is the property of all. Because human life only exists by being shared, all that is necessary for that life, for living and living well, is shared by the human family as a whole.

The traditional African idea of community seems to accord very closely with the understanding of human nature in contemporary Thomist philosophy presented above, which also avoids individualism by insisting on our dependence on other persons for our development. At the same time, it avoids the kind of collectivism criticised by the African thinkers by showing that it is only in strictly intersubjective relationships with others that we are able to grow as people.

The second African idea, that of *seriti*, denotes the peculiar value or dignity attaching to people as possessors of a kind of force or energy that manifests itself in human life and in the relations between persons, so that the world of human beings can be seen as a field of force in which individuals exist as focuses or vortices of the energy of the field. The striking thing about this from the point of view of European philosophy is that although *seriti* is not the kind of force that can be observed or measured by any instrument, it is not purely mental or spiritual either. Here is Setiloane's vivid attempt to describe it:

> The human person is like a live electric wire, which is ever exuding force or energy in all directions. The force that is thus exuded is called *seriti*. *Seriti* has often been translated to mean dignity or personality. Actually, that describes only the end result of the phenomenon. It is derived from the same word-stem *riti* as *moriti*, which means 'shadow' or 'shade'. It is a physical phenomenon which expresses itself externally to the human body in a dynamic manner. It is like an aura around the human person, an invisible shadow or cloud or mist forming something like a magnetic or radar field. It gives forth into the traffic or weltering pool of life in community the uniqueness of each person and each object. While physically its seat is understood to be inside the human body, in the blood, its source is beyond and outside of the human physical body . . . (1986, 13)

Such descriptions are clearly metaphorical and poetic attempts to describe something that is not simply either material or immaterial. The notion of *seriti* has in fact a sort of metaphysical function in African thought, and is used to explain the phenomena referred to by the expression *umuntu ngumuntu ngabantu*, the dependence of human beings on other people for personal growth. Setiloane again: '*Seriti* is not neutral. Its very existence seems calculated to promote and participate in relationship with the external world, human, animal, animate, inanimate, and even spiritual'. And even more explicitly:

> This manner of understanding human personality explains the interplay which takes place when people come into contact or live

together. The essence of being is 'participation', in which humans are always interlocked with one another. The human being is not only 'vital force', but more: 'vital force in participation'. The all-important principle is this 'vital participation' which forms the very soul of the community body and accounts for the miasma which attaches to the group, the clan or the tribe. 'Participation' with its concomitant element of 'belonging' is made possible by '*seriti*', which is ever engaged in interplay with other people's *diriti* whenever they come into contact. (Setiloane 1986, 14)

Such descriptions make it quite clear that interpersonal transactions are seen as depending on a kind of energy that, while not physical in any scientific sense, is not purely spiritual either. Thus it has a remarkable similarity to the kind of 'personal causality' that manifested itself in the Thomist account of intersubjective relationships between persons, an influence that is not physical in any way, or observable and measurable by any science, but is nonetheless certainly real.

If, therefore, we are able to build an ethics on the foundation of a contemporary Thomist conception of human nature, there is good reason to suppose that it would not be foreign to an African cultural context.

A contemporary philosophical ethic

The contemporary Thomist account of human nature presents people as the self-determining subjects of thought and action. It also depicts them as dependent on their environment, especially as constituted by other people, in all sorts of ways. Finally it reveals the special way in which we are dependent on other persons for the exercise, development and fulfillment of those capacities we possess precisely as persons and subjects.

The essence of the moral life in this view is the development and fulfillment of our human nature, especially our nature as persons, that is, as self-determining subjects of thought and action. As we have seen, however, this is only possible through certain kinds of relationships between persons, namely those in which self-knowledge and self-affirmation are developed. Together these make for a strictly intersubjective community of persons. Personal growth and personal community go hand in hand. Neither is possible without the other, and together they constitute the goal and the ultimate principle of morality.

With this conception of human nature as a foundation, it is not too difficult to construct a conceptual framework for the moral life. The various powers and tendencies of human nature are centred on and united in our power of self-realisation, our subjectivity. It is this above all that is the indicator of our moral character. If the moral life consists in the fulfillment of our human nature, it is this power, especially, that has to be developed. We can fail at other tasks without ruin; to fail at this is to destroy ourselves.

The idea of self-realisation is both general and abstract. We can however quickly make it more concrete. The self of which we are speaking is constituted by the capacities that make up our human nature. There are three sets or systems of such capacities: cognitive, volitional and emotional. Self-realisation consists in the development and integration of these systems in a goal-directed life.

In the cognitive sphere, self-realisation consists in the growth of our self-awareness into ever-fuller self-knowledge. In the volitional sphere, we must develop our capacity for self-determination into ever more complete self-affirmation. Both self-knowledge and self-affirmation are centred on the emotional system of the self. Self-knowledge consists fundamentally in knowing what our wants are and their order of importance in our lives. Self-affirmation consists fundamentally in promoting our desires to decisions in accordance with their value.

Self-knowledge is thus the principle of order and unity within each system of the self, in the cognitive sphere ranking our beliefs about what is desirable in order of importance so that this ranking can be reproduced in the volitional and emotional spheres in our decisions and desires. Self-affirmation is the principle of order and unity between the systems, ordering our decisions and ultimately our desires in conformity with this ranking. Thus, together, self-knowledge and self-affirmation are principles of integration of the self in its progress towards self-realisation.

If we understand human nature in this way, self-realisation can only come about under a certain kind of influence of other persons. To grow in self-knowledge and self-affirmation, I must be known and affirmed by others who both know and affirm themselves. Through their knowledge and affirmation of me, they enable me to know and affirm them, and through my knowledge and affirmation of them, I am able to know and affirm myself. We are thus bound in a circle of mutual affirmation.

Thus in this way we are able to derive from an insight into the subjectivity of human nature and the necessary conditions for its realisation in human life, a conceptual framework for an ethics, comprising a concrete ideal of individual character, of interpersonal relations and community.

In such an ethical task, the sciences will also have a role to play. Each of the social sciences will have something to contribute regarding the kind of social environment that would foster rather than hinder interpersonal transactions of the kind that bring about personal growth and community.

Ethics in an African context

I have tried to show how a particular philosophical understanding of human nature can act as the foundation for ethics. In doing so I have drawn on the work of contemporary philosophers who seek to bring about a return to the classical European tradition of moral philosophy, as well as contemporary Thomists influenced by existential and phenomenological philosophy.

What I (and the authors mentioned above) hope to achieve is a renewal of the tradition that leads from biblical and Greek ethical thought through Aquinas to the present day. This is the tradition that seeks to link ethics to the facts of human nature on one hand, and the forms of community produced by persons in the course of human history, on the other hand. I have suggested that there is much in common between a Thomist understanding of human nature and that contained in some traditional African ideas. This similarity extends to the sphere of morality as well.

In my treatment of the idea of *seriti*, I concentrated on the role it plays in the understanding of human nature and community. But it also has an ethical function. In traditional African thought morality is never merely conventional. As Tempels makes clear, 'Objective morality to the Bantu [*sic*] is ontological, immanent and intrinsic morality'. The fundamental norm in the ethics of traditional African thought is human nature itself: 'it is the living *muntu* who, by divine will, is the norm of either ontological or natural law' (1959, 121). It is in fact a natural law kind of ethics. And, as this nature is understood in terms of *seriti*, of vital force, so the moral life in all its individual, social and political ramifications is understood as the struggle to increase the power of this force. 'The activating and final aim of all Bantu [*sic*] effort is only the intensification of vital force. To protect or increase vital force, that is the motive and the profound meaning in all their practices.

It is the ideal which animates the life of the *muntu*, the only thing for which he [or she] is ready to suffer and to sacrifice himself [or herself]' (175).

In the period of colonialism and even more in the period of apartheid, this tradition was driven underground. But now in post-apartheid South Africa, it has re-emerged in all its moral richness. The notion of *ubuntu* that is the foundation of this ethic is more thoroughly dealt with by others in this book. I simply want to stress the fact that the foundation of this ethic is an understanding of human nature, its capacities and needs. The moral life is essentially connected with human flourishing; this idea permeates every aspect of the indigenous cultures of southern Africa.

The ethical theory I have outlined would be quite at home in such a cultural context, in which the good of the individual and of the group are inextricably intertwined. Of course, one has to remember that the social context of the moral life in South Africa is no longer that in which traditional African thought developed, but one formed and dominated by European science and technology. The institutions and practices that embodied and expressed traditional moral values and ideals are changing. A sympathetic reformulation of these ideals and values achieved on the basis of a dialogue between a traditional African outlook and the kind of European philosophical ethics I have presented can only help to make such changes creative ones.

A philosophical ethics of the kind that I have outlined above would also have a direct application to the process of nation-building that is going on in South Africa. However one envisages the goals – in the different dimensions of our life – of this process, it must be seen as one aimed at a more fully human social order, a society in which all people are able to develop to their full potential.

Such personal growth, moreover, is achieved (if the above account is accurate) only by means of the coming into being of a community of persons characterised by the fullest possible mutuality and reciprocity. It is a community, in short, that is a microcosm of social freedom, the freedom that is the positive side of the absence of domination and subjection, of any kind of conflict. Such an idea of human freedom, in which individual and social freedom are seen as necessarily interconnected, can provide an ethical standard with which to evaluate the aims, means and conduct of a particular political process such as ours.

The practical task of ethics in a South African context is to critically evaluate the different institutional milieus in which human life is lived, namely those of family, language, gender, education, work, recreation, healthcare, government and religion, considering the actual institutions themselves, the practices associated with them and the way in which they are understood and justified. In each case, one will be asking how far personal growth and community are fostered or hindered by them, that is, whether they are genuinely liberating or not.

Select bibliography

Aquinas, T. 1989. *Summa Theologiae: A Concise Translation*, ed. T. McDermott. Westminster: Christian Classics.
Donceel, J. 1967. *Philosophical Anthropology*. New York: Sheed and Ward.
Johann, R. 1966. *The Meaning of Love*. New Jersey: Paulist.
———. 1975. 'Person, Community and Moral Commitment'. In *Person and Community*, ed. R. Roth, 155–75. New York: Fordham.
———. 1976. 'Freedom and Morality from the Standpoint of Communication'. In *Freedom and Value*, ed. R. Johann, 45–59. New York: Fordham.
Lonergan, B. 1957. *Insight*. London: Darton, Longman and Todd.
———. 1972. *Method in Theology*. London: Darton, Longman and Todd.
Luijpen, W. 1960. *Existential Phenomenology*. Pittsburgh: Duquesne.
MacIntyre, A. 1981. *After Virtue*. London: Duckworth.
McCabe, H. 1968. *Law, Love and Language*. London: Sheed and Ward.
Menkiti, I.A. 1979. 'Person and Community in African Traditional Thought'. In *African Philosophy: An Introduction*, ed. R.A. Wright, 157–68. New York: University Press of America.
Meynell, H. 1981. *Freud, Marx and Morals*. London: Barnes and Noble.
Nedoncelle, M. 1966. *Love and the Person*. Trans. Sister Ruth Adelaide S.C. New York: Sheed and Ward.
Rahner, K. 1969. *Hearers of the Word*. London: Sheed and Ward.
———. 1978. *Foundations of Christian Faith*. London: Darton, Longman and Todd.
Senghor, L. 1963. 'Negritude and African Socialism'. In *St. Anthony's Papers* No. 15, ed. K. Kirkwood, 16–22. Oxford: Basil Blackwell.
———. 1966. 'Negritude'. *Optima* 16: 1–8.
Setiloane, G. 1986. *African Theology*. Johannesburg: Skotaville.
Tempels, P. 1959. *Bantu Philosophy*. Paris: Presence Africaine.
Toner, J. 1968. *The Experience of Love*. Washington: Corpus.

2

Ubuntu and Harmony
An African Approach to Morality and Ethics

NHLANHLA MKHIZE

THE IDEA OF *ubuntu*, or in Sotho *botho*, is central to an understanding of morality and ethics in African philosophy. This chapter advances the argument that to understand the idea of *ubuntu* and hence an African view of morality and ethics, it is important to begin with some ontological assumptions upon which ethics is grounded in traditional African thought. This is not to imply that ethics in traditional African thought is ontological. On the contrary, the traditional African view is that ethical concerns are practical and experiential; they cannot be separated from the lived experiences of the people in question. However, it is important to begin with ontological assumptions, as they underlie the ethical considerations to be discussed.

A number of these ontological assumptions have been discussed elsewhere (see Karenga 2004 and Mkhize 2004) and only a few are noted in this chapter. These are:

- the hierarchy of beings,
- God's essence or life force,
- the principle of cosmic unity,
- the principle of harmony, and
- the communal (relational) nature of being.

It can be argued that harmony is the overarching principle that glues all the other principles together. *Ubuntu*, the process of becoming an ethical human being, is the process by which balance or the 'orderedness of being' (Karenga

2004, 191) is affirmed. This is realised through relationships characterised by interdependence, justice, solidarity of humankind, respect, empathy and caring. Unethical conduct violates the orderedness of the cosmos. From this perspective, then, ethics is not a matter of individual legislation by abstract, solitary thinkers; rather, it is grounded in practical life and human action.

Ubuntu is not new. Similar concepts are found across Africa over many centuries, back to ancient times. In advancing the argument above, parallels can be drawn between the idea of *ubuntu* and the ancient African (Egyptian) concept of Maat (Karenga 2004). The idea of Maat, premised on similar ontological assumptions as *ubuntu*, emphasises harmony, righteousness and the need to locate and understand one's actions with reference to a larger whole. Obenga has noted similar parallels between ancient Egyptian and other African concepts (1989).

The hierarchy of beings

Traditional African moral and ethical systems can be said to be religious, in that they begin with the recognition of God as the omnipotent source of all life. Karenga notes that according to ancient African (Egyptian) mythology, God came into being as 'the bringer of being' (2004, 179) indicating that God is the source of all creation. Parallels can be drawn here with the Nguni (Zulu) idea of *Umvelinqangi*, literally, the One who emerged first, prior to the emergence of all creations.

However, it should be noted that in African mythology, God does not exist in complete isolation from the rest of creation. Rather, a hierarchy of beings is postulated, with God at the apex, and then at different levels, the living-dead (ancestors) as God's intermediaries, then human beings and then the rest of creation. People can communicate directly or indirectly with the living-dead (ancestors) (Mbiti 1991), who occupy the level immediately below God. In Zulu mythology, the world of the ancestors is divided into two (Ngubane 1977). First, there is the world of the recently deceased, who have to spend some time in the wilderness, while waiting for their relatives to perform the necessary rituals on their behalf, in order for them to proceed to the state of ancestorhood. Only integrated ancestors, those for whom rituals have been performed, are capable of communicating with God on behalf of their relatives. Ancestors, whose world is both analogous and contiguous to that of humans, continue to interact with, and remain interested in, the affairs of their relatives (Teffo and Roux 1998). Through acts of libation and sacrifices, a link is maintained with the ancestors, thereby ensuring a continued audience with God.

It should be further noted that not every person qualifies to be an ancestor in African thought. Rather, only those who have lived an exemplary life, a life characterised by high moral standards, proceed to ancestorhood. The most important standard is *ubuntu*, discussed below. Thus, ancestors are exemplars of good conduct and their superior moral qualities continue to be cherished. Ancestors also act as guardians of morality. While they generally remain interested in the well-being of their offspring, they punish bad conduct by withdrawing their interest in family matters. When this happens, having been disconnected from God, the source of life, the family is thrown into a state of imbalance or disequilibrium (Mkhize 2003). Such a state of affairs requires the family to engage in acts of libation in order to restore the state of equilibrium and hence connection to God. This highlights the dynamic conception of morality/ethics in traditional African thought: morality reflects harmony or the state of balance between people and their milieu. Where relationships have been thrown into disequilibrium, restoration is called for. This has several implications for countries such as South Africa, which have just emerged from a very violent past, a past characterised by total disregard of the humanity of others.

God's essence or life force
God is not apart from the rest of the world, but permeates everything in it; that is, all creations share in God's essence or life force. Karenga argues that 'the Creative source of Being' (God) is continuous; there is no ontological separation between God and the rest of creation because all manifestations are developments from the creator (2004, 195). According to Myers (1988), life force refers to the energy or power that is the essence of all phenomena, material and immaterial. Everything is endowed with God's energy or creative force. God not only created the world; She/He imbued it with divinity. Life force thus refers to dynamic creativity, thought to be the most precious gift from God. It is shared in descending order with ancestors, elders, human beings and all that is created (Kasenene 1994). The creativity of God's power is manifest in the changing seasons, birth, the cycles of nature, and in human achievements. The ethical implication of this is that because of this shared life force, human beings are expected

to live harmoniously with animals and nature in traditional African cosmology.

The principle of cosmic unity

Mutual sharing in the creative spirit eschews dualistic conceptions of the world. This means that there cannot be clear-cut distinctions between object and subject, self and other, given that we all share in God's creative energy. The idea of life force, discussed above, is predicated upon the notion of consubstantiation, which is the sharing of the substance of the whole with each of its parts (Myers 1988). Dualistic distinctions between mind and body (and between spirit and matter) do not make sense because everything is dependent upon, and shares in, another. The notion of being in harmony with one another and the universe, or consubstantiation, is best explained through the principle of cosmic unity.

Also known as a holistic conception of life, cosmic unity entails a connection between God, ancestors, animals, plants and inanimate objects, and everything that is created (see Mbiti 1991 and Verhoef and Michel 1997). Cosmic unity means that everything is perpetually in motion, influencing and being influenced by something else. From this perspective has evolved the view that knowing is a relational act. One does not know by standing and observing at a distance, unaffected. Knowing involves participation in the dynamic process, which involves interaction between parts and the whole (Mkhize 2003). From this belief emerges an ethic that prioritises social obligations to others, to one's community and to the cosmos in general. Individuals have to fulfill their duties and obligations to others and to the natural environment in order to maintain social equilibrium.

The principle of harmony or the 'orderedness of being'

The principle of harmony or balance (Myers 1988) – the 'orderedness of being', according to Karenga (2004, 191) – underpins the African conception of life and the universe. According to an African cosmology or worldview, argues Karenga, God's process of creation consisted of ordering existence from an unstructured or unordered reality to an orderly or harmonious state of being. The process of creation is thus an embodiment of order. The idea of life as order or balance is manifest in social justice, righteousness and truthfulness (Karenga 2004). It should be noted that the ideal state of affairs is an ordered or balanced one; human wrongdoing, unethical conduct or social injustice destabilises this order. Karenga suggests that

> within the concept of the orderedness of being is the concept of balance in the world; a balance that is constantly challenged by the negative ... and reaffirmed in the righteous acts (Maat) of humans ... Thus, the upholding of Maat [righteous acts] as order, rightness, and justice ... has ontological and ethical implications. And one is obligated to act accordingly for the benefit of society and the cosmos. (2004, 193)

The idea of order or harmony permeates a number of African conceptions of the world, such as the idea of health and illness (Ngubane 1977). For example, health does not simply mean the absence of disease; it incorporates balance and harmony between the individual and his or her social surroundings, including harmony with the self. Disease results from the breakdown in relatedness, including disharmony between the individual and the rest of the universe.

This idea of balance (harmony) as justice, respect, caring, and empathy is the foundation of the ethics of *ubuntu*. This is evident in Asante and Abarry's *African Intellectual Heritage*, in the section on Zulu personal decisions: 'To know the Law [righteousness] is the glory of being human: it is *ukuba ngumuntu*; perpetually to be responsible in *ukuba ngumuntu*' (1996, 378).

The communal/relational nature of being

In traditional African thought, human beings are born into a human society and hence the communitarian and concrete (as opposed to abstract) view of the self. Unlike Hobbesian subjects, who stand in isolation to define themselves as solitary, unattached thinkers, the human being in African thought defines the self with respect to the quality of his or her participation in a community of similarly constituted selves. Therefore, personhood is defined in relation to the community. The term 'community' refers to an organic relationship between individuals (Menkiti 1984). A sense of community exists if people are mutually responsive to one another's needs. As Karenga argues, 'a person is his character; or more definitively she is her *practice-in-relationships* as a result of her character. The motivation here, then, is not to enhance individualism or define and project individual rights, but to define relational obligations, the honoring of which gives one both her identity and sense of worth' (2004, 254; emphasis in original).

Mbiti summarises the importance attached to the community in self-definition using the dictum: 'I am because we are, and since we are, therefore I am' (1969, 214). Similarly, South African sayings such as *umuntu ngumuntu ngabantu* (Nguni) or *motho ke motho ka batho babang* (Sotho) point to this relational, interdependent view of the self. Roughly translated, these sayings mean that one attains the complements associated with full or mature selfhood through participation in a community of similarly constituted selves, a community of *abantu* (beings with moral sense). To be is to belong and to participate, it is to be born for the other (*muthu u bebelwa munwe*), as the Xhivenda saying maintains (Mkhize 2004).

There are parallels between the idea enunciated above of a being that is fully immersed in social relationships and the ancient Egyptian concept of Maat. According to Tobin, 'Maat was thus more than only the principle of universal order; it was an integral part, an inseparable aspect of the cosmos' (cited in Karenga 2004, 181). Karenga continues, 'Doing Maat, then, points toward locating and understanding oneself in the context of a larger whole and this has great significance for both social and environmental ethics. For to be a participant in such a context and process is an ongoing challenge to determine and maintain right relationships in the various spheres of activity and interaction which constitute the realm of being and becoming.'

The view that the ethics of *ubuntu*, like Maat, is premised on the idea of a fully immersed self is advanced below. Further, it can be shown that both *ubuntu* and Maat conceive of ethics in terms of connection, disconnection and restoration.

Ubuntu and the co-operative and ethical character of being

To be a human being (*ukuba ngumuntu*) is a social practice; it requires one to co-operate with others by doing good, thereby promoting the balance that is thought to characterise the universe. It requires human beings to live in solidarity with fellow human beings, their families, their communities, God and the rest of the world in which they find themselves. In some southern African languages, human beings who co-operate with others and the Divine are said to have *ubuntu* or *botho*.

This idea points to a being that is constantly in motion, as he/she engages with other people in order to maintain the orderedness of the cosmos, as I have argued elsewhere (Mkhize 2003). The word *ubuntu* is derived from the Nguni prefix *ubu-* and the stem *-ntu*. The prefix *ubu-* is reserved for a class of nouns that denote a process or a state of perpetual becoming. The stem *-ntu*, on the other hand, is reserved for human beings. Thus, the whole word, *ubu-ntu*, points to a being that is oriented toward becoming: it refers to an ongoing process that never attains finality. This process view of *umuntu* and hence *ubuntu*, finds support in Ramose who has argued that *umuntu* '*is the specific entity which continues to conduct an inquiry into experience, knowledge and truth*. This is an activity rather than an act. It is an ongoing process impossible to stop. On this reasoning, *ubu-* may be regarded as be-ing becoming and this evidently implies an idea of motion' (1999, 51; emphasis added).

Among the things that stand out in the quotation above is the idea that *umuntu* is a being in perpetual search of truth. *Ubu-ntu* (the process of becoming a human being), therefore, calls for a particular mode of being in the world. This mode of being requires each person to maintain social justice, to be empathetic to others, to be respectful to him/herself, towards others and the cosmos at large, and to have a conscience (*unembeza*) (Mkhize 2003). When these qualities of *ubuntu* are in place, social equilibrium is maintained. Failure to observe them disrupts communal unity, leading to disequilibrium. For this reason, Verhoef and Michel (1997) refer to this as a circular moral process. In a circular process, the community is always in a state of flux: it is strengthened if people fulfil their mutual obligations. Moral transgressions weaken the community by causing separation between people. However, separation resulting from moral transgression could be rectified if the community works interactively to re-establish social connection, interdependence and hence, communal unity (Verhoef and Michel 1997). Thus, human action is geared toward reconstructing, preserving and enhancing the community.

Karenga advances a similar view concerning the ethical and co-operative nature of being. The parallels between *ubuntu* and the idea of Maat, which Karenga postulates to be an ancient African (Egyptian) idea of ethics, are quite striking, both in terms of the process view of ethics and the view that *ubuntu* (ethics) incorporates justice, truth-seeking and fairness, as argued by Mkhize (2003). Karenga opines that Maat (righteousness):

is . . . also the cosmic glue that holds the world together that gives it meaning and motion. It is thus an ongoing project and product which must be constantly realized . . . And it is in this world maintenance project that humans collaborate and cooperate with the Divine. The relationship is a reciprocal one in which the Creator who brought being into being requires Maat [righteousness] from the living, so that he [or she] may live by it and that the world and existence itself may be maintained. (2004, 200)

Karenga continues, 'It is through this interpretation of real being as becoming that an anthropology of becoming takes shape. Thus, extending the existent becomes both an ontological and an anthropological process and imperative. For existence depends on the presence of Maat and humans are morally obligated to speak it and do it so that it is maintained and increased in the world' (202).

Thus, *ubuntu*, like Maat, captures the understanding that morality or ethics is an indispensable part of personhood. To be a fully moral person, one needs to belong. Belonging is not synonymous with group membership; it requires one to conduct oneself in a manner befitting of a fully moral being (*umuntu*), maintaining social justice, respectfulness and truthfulness, and being empathic towards others, among other attributes.

Ubuntu and individual rights

The view of ethics emerging from the ideas discussed above is not abstract or individualistic; rather, it is based on social relationships and practices. It is communitarian and existentialist. This is in contrast with approaches to ethics with which we have become familiar in much modern writing, approaches that presuppose free and autonomous individuals reasoning from an 'an original position' or 'behind a veil of ignorance' (Rawls 1972, 12). *Ubuntu* requires that ethics be reconceptualised. An African approach to ethics is not concerned with principles that have been abstracted from their social context. Rather, it is concerned with the phenomenological or lived experiences of the people in question.

By way of illustration perhaps, the distinction between *techne* and *phronesis* will help elucidate the approach to ethics advanced here (Gadamer 1975). *Techne* refers to the habitual application of rules and principles according to a predetermined plan: it is technical knowledge. *Phronesis*, on the other hand, is practical-moral knowledge, the ethical-moral knowledge required to make context-sensitive judgments. Unlike *techne*, which is something that one knows apart from oneself, *phronesis* is an important part of one's being or selfhood. Gadamer argues that the *phronimos* 'does not know and judge as one who stands apart and unaffected; but rather as one united by a specific bond with the other' (1987, 288). Like *phronesis*, the ethic of *ubuntu* is an integral aspect of being a human being. It is not something that one knows in an abstract sense; rather, it requires us to be fully aware of our social surroundings and to discharge our duties and obligations to others and the natural environment in general, thereby contributing towards the orderedness of being. The concept of *ubuntu* has far-reaching implications, given the social injustices that have become synonymous with many contemporary societies. The ethics of *ubuntu* is a call to action because an ethical being (*umuntu* – a being with moral sense) cannot look on the suffering of another and remain unaffected.

Conclusion

It has been argued that moral and ethical reasoning in African thought are premised on ontological assumptions such as the hierarchy of beings, the idea of life force, the principle of cosmic unity, the orderedness of being, and the communal view of being. Furthermore, *ubuntu*, like the ancient Egyptian concept of Maat, incorporates ideas of social justice, righteousness, care, empathy for others and respect. The ethic of *ubuntu* is an integral part of becoming: it cannot be separated from the self. It presupposes that good knowledge is not imposed from above, but is rather constructed socially and communally through social negotiation. Further, good knowledge maintains the social equilibrium or balance of the human group and the cosmos as a whole. Immorality results from the breakdown of the relationships between people and between people and the rest of the living world in which they live and interact. *Ubuntu* conceptualises ethical reasoning dynamically, in terms of human action, disequilibrium, and the restoration of harmony.

Select bibliography

Asante, M.K. and A.S. Abarry (eds.). 1996. *African Intellectual Heritage: A Book of Sources*. Philadelphia: Temple University Press.

Gadamer, H-G. 1975. *Truth and Method*. New York: Continuum.

———. 1987. 'The Problem of Historical Consciousness'. In *Interpretive Social Science: A Second Look*, eds. P. Rabinow and W.M. Sullivan, 103–60. California: University of California Press.

Karenga, M. 2004. *Maat: The Moral Ideal in Ancient Egypt: A Study in Classical African Ethics*. New York: Routledge.

Kasenene, P. 1994. 'Ethics in African Theology'. In *Doing Ethics in Context: South African Perspectives*, eds. C. Villa-Vicencio and J.W. de Gruchy, 138–47. New York: Orbis Books.

Mbiti, J.S. 1969. *African Religions and Philosophy*. London: Heinemann. 2nd edition, 1991.

Menkiti, I.A. 1984. 'Person and Community in Traditional African Thought'. In *African Philosophy: An Introduction*, ed. R.A. Wright, 171–81. Lanham, MD: University Press of America.

Mkhize, N. 2003. 'Culture and the Self in Moral and Ethical Decision-making: A Dialogical Approach'. Ph.D. dissertation, University of Natal, Pietermaritzburg.

———. 2004. 'Psychology: An African Perspective'. In *Critical Psychology*, eds. D. Hook, N. Mkhize, P. Kiguwa and A. Collins, 24–52. Cape Town: University of Cape Town Press.

Myers, L.J. 1988. *Understanding an Afrocentric World View: Introduction to an Optimal Psychology*. Dubuque, IA: Kendall/Hunt Publishing.

Ngubane, H. 1977. *Body and Mind in Zulu Medicine: An Ethnographic Study of Health and Disease in Nyuswa-Zulu Thought and Practice*. London: Academic Press.

Obenga, T. 1989. 'African Philosophy of the Pharonic Period'. In *Egypt Revisited*, ed. I. van Sertima, 286–324. New Brunswick: Transaction Publishers.

Ramose, M.B. 1999. *African Philosophy through Ubuntu*. Harare: Mond Books.

Rawls, J. 1972. *A Theory of Justice*. Oxford: Clarendon Press.

Teffo, L.J. and A.P.J. Roux. 1998. 'Metaphysical Thinking in Africa'. In *Philosophy from Africa: A Text with Readings*, eds. P.H. Coetzee and A.P.J. Roux, 134–48. Halfway House: International Thomson Publishing.

Verhoef, H. and C. Michel. 1997. 'Studying Morality within the African Context: A Model of Oral Analysis and Reconstruction'. *Journal of Moral Education* 26: 389–407.

3

Religious Ethics, HIV and AIDS and Masculinities in Southern Africa

EZRA CHITANDO

THE HIV AND AIDS pandemic has wreaked havoc in sub-Saharan Africa. It is the leading cause of death in southern Africa, with South Africa, Botswana and Zimbabwe having among the highest rates of infection in the world. The economically active and productive age group is being decimated and millions of children have already been orphaned. The task of caring for such orphans is increasingly falling on the sagging shoulders of grandmothers. HIV and AIDS have brought suffering, despair and death to a region that was full of promise, following successful struggles for liberation. This pandemic threatens the future of millions of people, and challenges the popular image of the youth as the leaders of tomorrow: 'in Botswana, South Africa and Zimbabwe an estimated 60 per cent of the young men who today are 15 years old will be infected with HIV during the course of their lifetimes, if prevention efforts do not succeed' (Weinrich and Benn 2004, 8).

This chapter seeks to utilise ethical insights from African traditional religion and Christianity in the struggle against HIV and AIDS in southern Africa. Its central focus is to invite reflection on the impact of masculinities on the spread of HIV in the region. It is informed by the conviction that the participation of men in HIV and AIDS prevention and awareness programmes is vital. It also seeks to draw attention to the importance of religion as a resource in fighting HIV and AIDS. Although communities of faith suffered from paralysis of analysis and theological timidity in the initial phase of the pandemic, there is a growing awareness that religion can play a meaningful role in facing the challenge. This chapter seeks to derive liberating principles from African traditional religion and Christianity to guide behavioural changes among men in the region. The two religious traditions provide ethical injunctions that can encourage men to adopt safer sexual practices and to participate in caregiving for people living with HIV and AIDS (PLWHA).

Religion and ethics in Africa: An overview
Before examining the role of religious ethics in transforming masculinities in southern Africa, it is necessary to highlight emerging perspectives on the interplay between religion and ethics. The academic community remains sharply divided over the nature of the relationship between religion and ethics. There are scholars who maintain that it is religion that provides the basis for ethical reflections, while there are others who make a fine distinction between morality and ethics, although the terms are often used interchangeably. Peter Kasenene explains that whereas ethics refers to principles of behaviour, morality focuses on the behaviour itself. Thus, 'in short, ethics is a reflection on morality; its nature, its presuppositions and its applications' (1998, 8).

The debate on religion and ethics in Africa follows a pattern that is also observable elsewhere in the world. In general, scholars who have religious backgrounds and operate within religious studies maintain that religion and ethics are conjoined. On the other hand, scholars trained in philosophy tend to argue that the study of ethics is an autonomous field. Although these two schools postulate diametrically opposed interpretations of the relationship between religion and ethics, it is possible to chart a middle path where certain ethical principles are seen as derived from religion, without having to subsume all ethics under religion.

John S. Mbiti, a leading African theologian and scholar of African traditional religion, has been chiefly responsible for the argument that religion is the basis for all ethical considerations in Africa. His basic thesis is that the African perception of reality is essentially and primarily religious. Throughout his career, Mbiti has repeatedly maintained that religion permeates all aspects of African existence. For him, the African is by nature *homo religiosus*, a religious person. To be is to be religious, Mbiti argues, with reference to Africa. It is religion that constitutes the hermeneutical key for understanding all other aspects of African life. Consequently, African societies do not make the distinction between the religious and the secular or between the sacred and the profane. There is no dimension of African life that is not influenced by religion, Mbiti argues. It follows therefore that morality and ethics in Africa should be understood through the lens of religion. Concerning African religion, Mbiti writes: 'it is by far the richest part of the African heritage. Religion is found in all areas of human life. It has dominated the thinking of African peoples to such an extent that it has shaped their cultures, their social life, their political organizations and economic activities' (1975, 9).

Mbiti's formulation that religion is the basis for interpreting African life has held sway in the study of religion in Africa for a long time. It has been reinforced by African theologians and historians of Christianity in Africa in their accounts of the massive conversions of Africans to Christianity. The view that Africans are characterised by a religious orientation has also been bolstered by anthropologists who seek to highlight the changing nature of indigenous religions. In the specific case of the relationship between religion and ethics in Africa, most contributors have endorsed the primacy of religion. Kasenene repeats Mbiti's formulation:

> Africans are very religious people and religion constitutes their way of life, influencing their physical, material, social or political concerns. All individual and group activities are religiously determined. At the same time, religion presents a corporate religiosity in the sense that it is not clearly differentiated from other modes of behaviour. It embraces the total life of the people and is integrated in all their institutions. The religious and the secular interpenetrate, to a greater or lesser degree, at all points of existence. In whatever an African does or experiences, there is a simultaneous working of spiritual and worldly forces. Thus, one cannot separate religion from morality. (1998, 18)

I have cited Kasenene at considerable length here because he represents the dominant position on the interface between religion and ethics within African religious studies. From the premise that religion is the foundation of the African worldview, the conclusion is drawn that ethics derive from religion. This argument appears sound, particularly in the context of the dominance of religion in Africa. In this view, morality would be seen as a consequence of the declarations of God, the ancestors or other spiritual beings. Interactions among individuals, as well as with their environment, are based on religious prescriptions.

While the position that seeks to maintain an intrinsic relationship between religion and ethics remains dominant, it has come under increasing scrutiny. The notion that religion permeates all dimensions of African existence has been criticised as being romantic. Some critics contend that secularism has become a reality in Africa. African philosophers, in particular, have charged that this religious view does not do justice to the intellectual abilities of Africans. Kwasi Wiredu, a Ghanaian philosopher, has sought to separate religion and morality in his writing. He admits that religion no longer appeals to him and he seeks to identify alternative interpretations of reality. According to him, 'in the Akan scheme of things morality is not attached to religion either in its conception or in its practice' (1983, 12). Wiredu argues that a number of contemporary studies of traditional African philosophies of morals converge on the point that religion and morality constitute autonomous spheres. Thus, 'communalistic rules of conduct are a clear extension of the imperatives of pure morality. Since both are defined in terms of human interests, the African ethic might be called humanistic, as opposed to supernaturalistic. This contradicts the widely received notion that in Africa morality logically depends upon religion' (Wiredu 2004, 18).

Kasenene and Wiredu might be taken as representatives of the opposing schools of thought that have emerged in relation to the question of whether, and how, religion and ethics interact in Africa. The African religionist school, within which Kasenene is located, emphasises the centrality of religion to Africa. Scholars operating within this paradigm insist that it is religion that constitutes a guide to belief and action in Africa. Religious ethics therefore define ethical reflections in Africa, hence the title of Kasenene's book, *Religious Ethics in Africa* (1998). As the overwhelming majority of scholars within African faculties of theology or departments of religious studies hold religious beliefs themselves (Cox 1994, 3), they tend to see religion as playing an important role in African ethics. Scholars such as Bolaji Idowu, Laurenti Magesa, Tom J. Obengo and others have highlighted the primary role of religion in African ethical reflections.

The African philosophical school, to which Wiredu belongs, seeks to separate religion from ethics. Scholars such as Kwame Gyekye feel that religion has not been helpful to Africa's struggle for scientific advancement (see 1997, 245). These scholars argue that it is simplistic to regard religion as the basis for morality in Africa. Other African philosophers concede that religion is an important factor in Africa, but interpret religion in humanistic terms and regard the African religionist emphasis on religion as misplaced. Thus:

> In essence, it is being suggested here that religion developed out of a human necessity and served the human need for knowledge and security. The injunctions of morality, insofar as they are related to religion in an African environment, will be found to be motivated by humanistic considerations. Thus the invocation of the Supreme Being, the divinities, the ancestors and other forces in moral matters is mainly intended to lend legitimacy, through an already available reinforcement mechanism, to what is often taken for granted as morally obligatory in a humanistic sense. Being morally upright is not as much a matter of pleasing the supernatural forces as it is of promoting human welfare (Bewaji 2004, 398–99)

Unlike the religionists, many African philosophers do not operate from a religious perspective, with the exception of those from the Catholic Church. African Catholic philosophers, such as Benezet Bujo, are primarily religionists in their orientation. Secularist African philosophers effectively question the value of religion to Africa, even as they maintain that religion and ethics are not logically related. Scholars such as Wiredu, Gyekye and Bewaji cited above do not share the religionists' assumption that religion is at the core of ethics in Africa. They consider such a position unconvincing, and emerging from a failure to understand the humanistic character of African communities. They argue that the contention that religion permeates all aspects of life, although endorsed in other religious traditions, such as Hinduism and Islam, robs the concept of analytical content. In this regard, African philosophers have a valid point for positing alternative sources for African ethics. On the other hand, African religionists have been convincing in their descriptions of those aspects of African ethics that derive from religion. They have shown how the ancestors are believed to have put forward rules and regulations to govern human behaviour, and how this has shaped actual human behaviour.

This debate over the interface between religion and ethics in Africa exposes hidden tensions within African scholarship. It requires a longer narrative to fully explore the intricacies involved in the discourses on religion and ethics in Africa. In a separate study, I have highlighted some of the limitations of the religionist position (see Chitando 1997). Perhaps the dilemma posed by African religionists and philosophers is a false one. One does not need to identify religion as the source of *all* ethical principles in order to highlight the importance of religious ethics. It is within this context that this chapter seeks to steer a middle path between these positions by paying attention to religious ethics that could be used in the struggle against HIV and AIDS in southern Africa. The humanistic reductionism put forward by Wiredu and Bewaji does not threaten our position in a convincing manner. Whether or not religion is a human invention, this factor does not dilute the fact that some ethical precepts can be usefully drawn from the domain of religion. Since most Africans do in fact hold quite firm religious beliefs, it is wise not to ignore the effect of these beliefs or their persuasive power.

Masculinities and HIV and AIDS in southern Africa

The debate on religion and ethics is relevant to the discussion on masculinities in southern Africa, since religious and cultural factors have reinforced emerging ideas of what it means to be a man. The high status enjoyed by a boy child is a direct outcome of religious ideas that project him as the one responsible for perpetuating the ancestral lineage. Cultural factors are responsible for shaping male sexual behaviour, while patriarchal ideologies justify ethical choices made by men. Although African philosophers are right to insist that religion does not explain everything relating to ethics in African contexts, in the paragraphs below, I seek to highlight the extent to which cultural and religious factors influence the formation and performance of hegemonic masculinities. In addition, I shall argue that these masculinities have been a major factor in the spread of HIV.

The spread of HIV and AIDS in southern Africa has followed some fault lines that were already in existence prior to the outbreak of the pandemic. From the late 1980s, HIV and AIDS have spread rapidly throughout the region, with life expectancy falling to 47 years, from a previous high of 62 years (Weinrich and Benn 2004, 8). While theorists continue to grapple with the important question of the origin(s) of HIV, most activists contend that the most pressing task now should be in the direction of prevention and care. This is critical in a region where HIV and AIDS have affected socially disadvantaged populations. According to Musa Dube, a biblical studies scholar and activist from Botswana, these populations already 'face poverty, gender inequality, violence, international injustice, racism, ethnic conflict, denial of children's rights, [and] discrimination on the basis of sexual orientation and ethnicity' (2003b, 11). Although this chapter concentrates on the deconstruction of masculinities, it is important to bear in mind that the spread of HIV is directly related to structural inequalities, historical precedents and cultural politics. This from Weinrich and Benn:

> From our own and others' collective research, it is clear that AIDS has been exacerbated by deepening poverty experienced by the majority of African countries over the past twenty years; that it has spread in the aftermath of war, civil unrest, and refugee movements; that migration patterns necessitated by underemployment in chronically underfinanced economies ensure both an increase in the rates of transmission and a spread from urban to rural areas; and that governments shackled by poor terms of trade and crippling debts have neither the finances nor the personnel to address the problem adequately. (2004, 5)

It is within this context of multiple disadvantages that populations in the region face the reality of gender inequality, a vital factor for understanding the spread of HIV and AIDS. Young women are more likely to be infected than their male counterparts, for a number of reasons. Most analysts attribute this to physiological differences and socio-economic factors. Thus, 'many factors are involved (such as women's greater anatomical and physical vulnerability to the transmission of HIV), but most come down to the ways in which African women and girls are socially subordinate to, and economically dependent upon, men' (Farley 2004, 136).

Gender inequalities in southern Africa are reinforced by notions of masculinity that are dominant in the region. These masculinities have endangered both women and men and are often buttressed by religious and cultural ideologies. While being male is a biological factor, the process of expressing manhood is informed by social, cultural and religious factors. It is therefore important to acknowledge that socialisation plays a major role in the performance of masculine identities. As Robert Morrell argues, masculinities are fluid. Furthermore, 'they are socially and historically constructed in a process which involves contestation between rival understandings of what being a man should involve' (2001, 7).

Although individual men are directly responsible for their actions, entire communities are implicated in the development and deployment of masculinities. The choices that are available to specific individuals are socially circumscribed. In addition, most theorists have overlooked the extent to which women usually consent to, and are often co-producers of, masculinities. This may be illustrated from the domain of sexuality where boys are taught to take the lead, while girls are expected to be passive. These socially defined expectations are usually played out, with most young men appearing to be more knowledgeable sexually. However, these identities need to be interrogated in the context of HIV and AIDS.

Patriarchal and religious ideologies have coagulated to form masculinities that have led to gender oppression in southern Africa. Missionary religions such as Christianity and Islam have worsened the situation by promoting an image of men as the divinely ordained leaders of their communities. In addition, although women played active roles in the struggles for liberation, masculine identities have been emphasised in the post-colonial situation. As Horace Campbell has illustrated, with reference to Zimbabwe, a very patriarchal system of governance has emerged (2003). Liberation leaders such as Robert Mugabe and Sam Nujoma of Namibia have been portrayed as 'Fathers of the Nation' or 'Messianic Deliverers', who have led their people to the 'Promised Land'. However, their pronouncements against homosexuality are based on their interpretation of what so-called 'real men' should do, that is, have sexual relations with women. Mugabe has called for the emergence of 'real men' (*amadoda sibili*) in his Cabinet (Gundani 2002, 154). Nationalist rhetoric presents an interesting arena where the deployment of specific masculinities has been encouraged. 'Real men' are supposed to be fearless, daring, and to have a macho image. These identities are problematic in contexts of HIV and AIDS, as I shall elaborate below.

The notion of a man as a sexual predator has had disastrous consequences in southern Africa. Cultural factors have led many men to regard themselves as having uncontrollable sexual urges and many have multiple sexual partners. Men in the military, truck drivers, and those in activities that perpetuate specific notions of masculinity have often engaged in risky sexual behaviours. The preoccupation with virility has led many older men to court younger women. A Zimbabwean study shows how some older men abuse their economic power to force adolescent girls into engaging in transactional sex (Chinake, Dunbar and Van Der Straten 2002).

Masculinities are also responsible for the definition of sex as penetration by the male organ. Other possible definitions, such as the traditional Swazi prescription that a boy could make love to his fiancée between her thighs while avoiding penetration (Kasenene 1998, 60) have been replaced by the preoccupation with penetration. The image of a real man as one who undertakes risky ventures has also frustrated efforts to promote the use of condoms. Some men demand 'live' sex and maintain that condoms are for cowards. In some instances, the presence of sexually transmitted infections has been celebrated as the mark of maleness. In her research in South African mining compounds, Catherine Campbell notes that masculinities were central to shaping sexual behaviour: 'linked to this masculine identity were the repertoires of insatiable sexuality, the need for multiple sexual partners, and a manly desire for the pleasure of flesh-to-flesh sexual contact' (2004, 151).

The masculinities outlined above have had extremely unfortunate consequences for women in southern Africa. Most married women have been infected by their husbands, since they have had sex solely with their husbands (Shisana 2004, 6). Writing from a South African context, theologians Tinyiko S. Maluleke and Sarojini Nadar maintain that religion, culture and gender socialisation have formed an 'unholy trinity' or 'covenant of death' against women in Africa (2002). While society continues to preach the message of abstinence, faithfulness and condom use, African women are suffocating under oppressive masculinities. Men have largely abused religious and cultural resources to continue engaging in risky sexual behaviour, while dangerously exposing their partners to HIV.

Apart from compromising HIV and AIDS prevention and awareness programmes, masculinities in southern Africa have also curtailed the participation of most men in the provision of care to PLWHA. In many cases, infected wives have taken care of their husbands up to the point of death, only for there to be no one take care of them when they fall ill themselves. In addition, masculinities define male illness as more important, since the man is projected as the breadwinner, despite the fact that many women earn as much as, or in some cases, more than their husbands. The situation of African women in the provision of care for PLWHA is a sad one indeed, as Farley points out:

> In addition to being sexually vulnerable, women consistently bear the greater share of caregiving for those who are affected by or infected with HIV. It is women who care for the sick and for the orphans; it is women who must see to the dying. At the same time women in sub-Saharan Africa (as in the world generally) do not have the economic, social and political power that is needed for effective responses to HIV/AIDS. (2004, 137)

Cultural factors have allowed men to have minimal roles in the provision of care to PLWHA. Home-based care programmes that have been implemented throughout the region are, in fact, women-based initiatives. Most men do not spend enough time at home to be in any position to provide quality care for those affected by or infected with HIV. Cultural and religious factors allow men to seek entertainment outside the home, leaving women and children to cope with the challenge of providing care. Preparing food, washing and providing company to PLWHA are all activities that are seen as the responsibility of women.

Stigma is another challenge that has emerged with HIV and AIDS in southern Africa. Religious interpretations of the disease have tended to associate it with punishment for sin and immorality on the part of those who are suffering. Perhaps the African philosophers have a valid point when they refuse to let religion play a role in formulating ethical principles in Africa. Some religious groups and individuals have been responsible for a lot of suffering through their teachings that HIV is a result of loose living. According to Dube, 'this perspective contributed towards creating a second epidemic, namely, stigma and discrimination of those with HIV/AIDS, intensifying the suffering of the infected and affected through social isolation, rejection, fear and hopelessness' (2003a, viii). Unfortunately, stigmatisation has followed gendered patterns, where women with HIV and AIDS are more likely to be exposed to stigma than men.

Masculinities are also implicated in the stigmatisation of women living with HIV and AIDS. Since the colonial period, there has been a tendency to portray women as carriers of disease. In Zimbabwe, African women who dared to access urban public space were labelled as 'stray', 'loose', 'dangerous' and other derogatory labels. In the contemporary period, young women have been portrayed as the source of the HIV and AIDS pandemic (Jackson 1999). Men have defined urban public space as their own exclusive domain, and women who transcend these boundaries are often castigated. It is from such biased perspectives that most women are held responsible for the deaths of their husbands of HIV and AIDS. Urban spaces in southern Africa are choking with oppressive masculinities and narratives of blame tend to heap on women, who are often powerless to protest their innocence.

In his study of unsolicited street remarks directed at women in Harare, socio-linguist Pedzisai Mashiri highlights the deeply entrenched masculinities that are at work in African urban contexts (2000). Young urban females are subjected to verbal and physical abuse by men who regard themselves as demi-gods. This pattern is replicated across the region, with the authorities paying little attention, as they are preoccupied with more 'manly' issues of governance. In their worst form, these masculinities find expression in the rape and abuse of women and children. Some men in institutions (military, police, education, church) have abused their socially more powerful positions to persuade or compel women to engage in sexual activities (Weinrich and Benn 2004, 31). It is a tragedy that a region that has the highest rates of HIV-infection is also recording a high incidence of rape.

The portrayal of women as objects for male sexual gratification and as carriers of disease is also discernible in popular songs and literature (Vambe 2003). In Zimbabwe, Leonard Zhakata, a popular musician, charged that female genital organs now resemble a poisoned well, thereby posing a danger to the whole community. Chenjerai Shire has examined how masculinities that are informed by assumed essential differences between men and women have led to gender discrimination. Men claim to have the licence to do as they please, since, unlike women, 'men don't go to the moon' (Shire 1994).

From the foregoing paragraphs, it is clear that masculinities play an important role in the spread of HIV in the region of southern Africa. Masculinities inform and facilitate the tendency by some men to have multiple sexual partners and not to use condoms, limit the participation of men in the provision of care for PLWHA and contribute to the stigmatising of women. It is therefore clear that there is need for introspection regarding the definitions of masculinities, since gender inequalities have worsened the HIV and AIDS pandemic. As results of successful awareness programmes from Uganda and Senegal have shown, behaviour change does have an impact on the spread of HIV and AIDS. Since individual men can do very little to change structural injustices in the short term, there is need to focus on the empowerment of individuals to undergo radical transformation in relation to their self-perception. A lot of work needs to be done if hegemonic masculinities are to be transformed.

Religious ethics and the transformation of masculinities in southern Africa

Although the masculinities described above are reinforced by appeals to religious and cultural ideologies, ethical ideals from religion could be used to transform them. Adopting a liberating perspective could allow men to play a strategic role in the struggle against HIV and AIDS.

In this chapter, I am proposing the concept of solidarity as an ethical imperative from African traditional religion and Christianity, which can be used to transform masculinities in southern Africa. This concept has had considerable currency within the region, having been used in liberation struggles against settler colonialism and apartheid. Socialist groups in Europe also adopted the concept of solidarity to capture their commitment to black resistance movements in the region. However, the concept is also firmly rooted in religious ethics, particularly within the liberationist paradigm. For example, Bujo alludes to the importance of solidarity in African ethics, but he does not undertake a detailed analysis (see 2001, 5–6).

Solidarity implies standing for, and standing with 'the Other'. It transcends sympathy and represents an existential transformation on the part of the one who commits himself or herself to stand with the suffering and the marginalised. In phenomenological parlance, solidarity emerges from the process of empathetic interpolation, where an individual endeavours to experience the world from the perspective of the one he or she seeks to understand. In relation to the discourse on masculinities, solidarity implies the willingness of men to be self-emptying and to stand with women in the battle against HIV and AIDS. Solidarity calls for self-reflection on the part of men in southern Africa, so that they interrogate their position of power and show that they can identify with the cries of pain from women and children.

The notion of solidarity is related to, but goes beyond, the philosophy of *ubuntu* that has received considerable attention in African philosophy. Scholars such as Augustine Shutte (2001) and others have examined the communitarian nature of African societies. They have emphasised the extent to which individualism is suppressed in favour of communal interests. Theo Sundermeier discusses this idea in relation to communal life and interdependence and argues that the notion of community in Africa extends to the environment. Thus, 'the life of individuals, their luck and the jealousy of their companions, their misfortune and the goodwill of others, have an effect on the weal and woe of the community and the fertility of the land' (Sundermeier 1998, 18).

Unfortunately, most African philosophical reflections on *ubuntu* or 'person and community' (Wiredu and Gyekye 1992) do not grapple with oppressive masculinities that lie behind these impressive concepts. How has it been possible for many African men to proclaim, 'I am, because we are' and then proceed to engage in risky sexual behaviour in the context of HIV and AIDS? Could it be that masculinities inform the very communitarian ideal that both African religionists and philosophers valorise? In reality, male-centred definitions of community have left women and children at the margins. Applying the concept of solidarity could result in more inclusive interpretations of the community.

As recent feminist studies of African traditional religion have shown, indigenous religions do accord space and respect to women (see, for example, Olajubu 2003). In terms of the implications of African traditional religion, men therefore have the responsibility of ensuring that they uphold the integrity of human life by not exposing their partners to HIV. According to indigenous teachings, to be in solidarity implies devoting oneself to the well-being of 'the Other'. Therefore the 'I', ego or self should no longer thirst for countless sexual encounters, but should be made subordinate to the interests of 'the Other'. Indigenous languages in the region articulate this spiritual truth through numerous proverbs, pithy sayings, folktales and other strategies.

The relationship between the spirits and humans provides a paradigmatic model for the solidarity that should guide interactions between men and women in Africa. According to African traditional religion, ancestral spirits are always in solidarity with their descendants, ensuring that they experience abundant life. Masculinities that promote this ideal should be based on solidarity with vulnerable women and children. Munyaradzi F. Murove has shown how the Shona concept of *ukama* governs human interactions (1999). One does not act in ways that endanger one's relatives. Rather, one is always seeking to enhance their quality of life. Men who are in solidarity with women should therefore engage in safer sexual practices. These include abstinence, faithfulness, using condoms, as well as reducing the number of their sexual partners and encounters.

Christianity also provides helpful guidelines relating to the role of solidarity in sexual ethics. While the central concern of Christianity has been to ensure individual spiritual salvation, it is possible to salvage alternative models that promote solidarity. Puleng LenkaBula, a South African theological ethicist, maintains that the unquestionable inviolability of human life is a salient feature of Christian sexual ethics (2002, 64). Society has a duty to value human life, a theme that resonates with the teachings of African traditional religion as summarised above. Since HIV and AIDS are a threat to human life, men are called upon to adopt responsible attitudes in the face of their devastating impact. Traditional Christian teachings of morality, although inadequate in the face of structural challenges, therefore remain useful. For example, Armin Zimmerman proposes new Christian sexual ethics that realistically considers the role of condoms (2004). Furthermore, Christian ethics espouse the idea of promoting closed sexual relationships. The concept of solidarity can empower men to forsake masculinities that promote multiple sexual partners and to identify with their partners.

Increasing male participation in caregiving and fighting stigma: The role of solidarity

Both African traditional religion and Christianity contain ethical values that illustrate how the concept of solidarity can be used to challenge gendered patterns of caregiving. They also have resources to undermine stigma and discrimination. According to Bujo, 'African ethics treats the dignity of the human person as including the dignity of the entire creation, so that the cosmic dimension is one of its basic components' (2001, 2). Having such a high regard for the dignity of the human person, societies in southern Africa need to weed out oppressive masculinities that stifle the full inclusion of women under the category of human persons. Stigma and discrimination against women is also tantamount to denying their status as full and worthy members of the community.

For men to be in solidarity with PLWHA, committed and persistent participation in caregiving is crucial. It is through giving up masculinities that confine caregiving to women that men in the region can demonstrate their commitment to those affected by and infected with HIV. The fundamental principle of African ethics is that solidarity and fellowship with others is the basis for becoming fully human. Thus: 'Behind this lies the view that the human person acts more effectively to the extent that he holds fast to *solidarity* with those like himself; for thus he [or she] raises the quality of the vital force not only for himself [or herself]; but rather for the entire community, indeed for the whole of humanity' (Bujo 2001, 5; emphasis added).

By seriously reflecting on the need to play an active role in the provision of care and providing relief to overburdened women, men can mitigate the effects of HIV and AIDS in southern Africa. Obviously, much advocacy work needs to be done in this regard. Both African traditional religion and Christianity have traditions that place emphasis on the prophetic model for instigating ethical revolutions. Prophets are individuals who make pronouncements in favour of the oppressed and the marginalised. They denounce injustice, while promoting health and well-being within their communities. In the face of hegemonic masculinities in southern Africa, it is clear that there is a need for prophets who will promote solidarity.

Solidarity in looking after those affected by and infected with HIV will lead men to interrogate their privileges under patriarchy. Too much injustice has persisted in the name of defending African culture. Why should ailing grandmothers be left to fetch water and firewood, while boys enjoy social soccer? Why should men engage in endless political bar talk, while women struggle to feed orphans and PLWHA? Gender roles are not cast in stone, nor are they divinely ordained. As I have argued throughout this chapter, they are socially constructed and are often consciously deployed. Consequently, they can be realigned.

As African women theologians such as Mercy Amba Oduyoye (1995) have observed, most African men hide under cultural arguments to gloss over gross injustices against women. Oppressive gender relations have been sanitised by appeals to African culture. However, both African traditional religion and Christianity promote a vision of providing abundant life to all their adherents in the life before death. The value of standing with vulnerable social groups should empower men to become combatants in the struggle against HIV and AIDS in the southern African region.

The respect for women and children that is promoted by progressive versions of African traditional religion and Christianity could lead a reduction in rape and sexual abuse. Men who are in solidarity with women are painfully aware of the effects of rape and sexual abuse. African traditional religion and Christianity call upon their adherents to side with those who are suffering. The ministry of Jesus provides the perfect model for those who seek to understand the ethics of solidarity. He always stood in solidarity with those who were on the margins of the society of his day – lepers, women, children, prostitutes and others. If the millions of Christians in southern Africa could live up to the Christian ethical injunction of loving one's neighbour, HIV and AIDS, and the associated stigma and discrimination would be reduced significantly.

For liberating masculinities that are based on solidarity to emerge, advocacy work has to be undertaken at personal, family, community, national and international levels. Parents, schools and communities need to inculcate new masculinities in boys and young men, so that they begin to appreciate the need for solidarity with women from an early age. The ethical revolution needs to begin early in life. Organisations that work in the areas of HIV and AIDS prevention and awareness should also pay more attention to the impact of masculinities in the spread of HIV. Religious organisations and theological training institutions should also empower learners to handle ethical issues relating to HIV and AIDS (Chitando 2002, 77).

Conclusion

While the struggle against HIV and AIDS should not be simplistically reduced to questions of personal morality, in this chapter, I have argued that masculinities that have been deployed in southern Africa have had an impact on the spread of HIV. Against some African philosophers who do not see a role for religion in ethical reflections in Africa, I have argued that African traditional religion and Christianity offer solidarity as a helpful resource for empowering men to overcome hegemonic masculinities. This could equip men to adopt safer sexual practices, increase participation in caregiving and help to overcome stigma and discrimination. Religious ethics might empower men to generate new and liberating models for expressing maleness in southern Africa. As a culture of death threatens to paralyse this region, solidarity and hope might revitalise communities and allow people to become more optimistic about the future.

Select bibliography

Bewaji, John A.I. 2004. 'Ethics and Morality in Yoruba Culture'. In *A Companion to African Philosophy*, ed. Kwasi Wiredu, 396–403. Oxford: Blackwell.

Bujo, Benezet. 2001. *Foundations of an African Ethic: Beyond the Universal Claims of Western Morality*. New York: The Crossroad Publishing Company.

Campbell, Catherine. 2004. 'Migrancy, Masculine Identities, and AIDS: The Psychosocial Context of HIV Transmission on the South African Gold Mine'. In *HIV and AIDS in Africa: Beyond Epidemiology*, eds. Ezekiel Kalipeni, Susan Craddock, Joseph R. Oppong and Jayati Ghosh, 144–54. Oxford: Blackwell.

Campbell, Horace. 2003. *Reclaiming Zimbabwe: The Exhaustion of the Patriarchal Model of Liberation*. Trenton, NJ: Africa World Press.

Chinake, Hazel, Megan Dunbar and Ariane van der Straten. 2002. 'Intergenerational Sex among Adolescents in Zimbabwe'. Abstract No. MoOrE1116. Fourteenth International Conference on AIDS, Barcelona 7–12 July.

Chitando, Ezra. 1997. 'A Curse of the Western Heritage? Imagining Religion in an African Context'. *Journal for the Study of Religion* 10 (2): 75–98.

———. 2002. 'HIV and AIDS Curriculum for Theological Institutions in Zimbabwe: An Exploratory Essay'. *Zimbabwe Journal of Educational Research* 14 (1): 72–93.

Cox, James L. 1994. 'Religious Studies by the Religious: A Discussion of the Relationship between Theology and the Science of Religion'. *Journal for the Study of Religion* 7 (2): 3–31.

Craddock, Susan. 2004. 'Introduction – Beyond Epidemiology: Locating AIDS in Africa'. In *HIV and AIDS in Africa: Beyond Epidemiology*, eds. Ezekiel Kalipeni, Susan Craddock, Joseph R. Oppong and Jayati Ghosh, 1–10. Oxford: Blackwell.

Dube, Musa W. 2003a. 'Introduction: Towards Multi-Sectoral Teaching in a Time of HIV/AIDS'. In *HIV/AIDS and the Curriculum: Methods of Integrating HIV/AIDS in Theological Programmes*, ed. Musa W. Dube, vii–xiii. Geneva: WCC Publications.

———. 2003b. 'Methods of Integrating HIV/AIDS in Biblical Studies'. In *HIV/AIDS and the Curriculum: Methods of Integrating HIV/AIDS in Theological Programmes*, ed. Musa W. Dube, 10–23. Geneva: WCC Publications.

Farley, Margaret A. 2004. 'Partnership in Hope: Gender, Faith, and Responses to HIV/AIDS in Africa'. *Journal of Feminist Studies in Religion* 20 (1): 133–48.

Gundani, Paul. 2002. 'The Land Crisis in Zimbabwe and the Role of the Churches towards its Resolution'. *Studia Historiae Ecclesiasticae* 28 (2): 122–69.

Gyekye, Kwame. 1997. *Tradition and Modernity: Philosophical Reflections on the African Experience.* New York: Oxford University Press.

Jackson, Lynette. 1999. '"Stray Women" and "Girls on the Move": Gender, Space, and Disease in Colonial and Post-Colonial Zimbabwe'. In *Sacred Spaces and Public Quarrels: African Cultural and Economic Landscapes*, eds. Ezekiel Kalipeni and Paul T. Zeleza, 146–67. Trenton, NJ: Africa World Press.

Kasenene, Peter. 1998. *Religious Ethics in Africa.* Kampala: Fountain Publishers.

LenkaBula, Puleng. 2002. 'From the Womb into the Hostile World: Christian Ethics and the Abuse of Children in South Africa'. *Journal of Theology for Southern Africa* 114: 55–68.

Maluleke, Tinyiko S. and Sarojini Nadar. 2002. 'Breaking the Covenant of Violence against Women'. *Journal of Theology for Southern Africa* 114: 5–17.

Mashiri, Pedzisai. 2000. 'Street Remarks, Address Rights and the Urban Female: Socio-Linguistic Politics of Gender in Harare'. *Zambezia* 27 (1): 55–70.

Mbiti, John S. 1975. *Introduction to African Religion.* London: Heinemann.

Morrell, Robert. 2001. 'Introduction – The Time of Change: Men and Masculinity in South Africa'. In *Changing Men in Southern Africa*, ed. Robert Morrell, 3–37. Pietermaritzburg: University of Natal Press.

Murove, Munyaradzi F. 1999. 'The Shona Concept of *Ukama* and the Process Philosophical Concept of Relatedness, with Special Reference to the Ethical Implications of Contemporary Neo-Liberal Economic Practices'. Masters thesis, University of Natal, Pietermaritzburg.

Obengo, Tom J. 1997. 'The Role of Ancestors as Guardians of Morality in African Traditional Religions'. *Journal of Black Theology in South Africa* 11 (2): 44–63.

Oduyoye, Mercy A. 1995. *Daughters of Anowa: African Women and Patriarchy.* Maryknoll, NY: Orbis Books.

Olajubu, Oyorenke. 2003. *Women in the Yoruba Religious Sphere.* New York: State University of New York Press.

Shire, Chenjerai. 1994. '"Men Don't Go to the Moon": Language, Space and Masculinities in Zimbabwe'. In *Dislocating Masculinity: Comparative Ethnographies*, eds. Andrea Cornwall and Nancy Lindisfarne, 147–58. New York: Routledge.

Shisana, Olive. 2004. 'Gender and HIV/AIDS: Focus on South Africa'. Paper delivered at the inaugural International Institute on Gender and HIV/AIDS, 7 June, South Africa.

Shutte, Augustine. 2001. *Ubuntu: An Ethic for a New South Africa.* Pietermaritzburg: Cluster Publications.

Sundermeier, Theo. 1998. *The Individual and Community in African Religions.* Hamburg: Lit Verlag.

Vambe, Maurice T. 2003. 'HIV/AIDS, African Sexuality and the Problem of Representation in Zimbabwean Literature'. *Journal of Contemporary African Studies* 21 (3): 473–88.

Weinrich, Sonja and Christoph Benn. 2004. *AIDS – Meeting the Challenge: Data, Facts, Background.* Geneva: WCC Publications.

Wiredu, Kwasi. 1983. 'Morality and Religion in Akan Thought'. In *Philosophy and Cultures: Proceedings of 2nd Afro-Asian Philosophy Conference, Nairobi, October/November, 1981*, eds. H. Odera Oruka and D.A. Masolo, 6–13. Nairobi: Bookwise Limited.
———. 2004. 'Introduction: African Philosophy in Our Time'. In *A Companion to African Philosophy*, ed. Kwasi Wiredu, 1–27. Oxford: Blackwell.
Wiredu, Kwasi and Kwame Gyekye. 1992. *Person and Community*. Ghanaian Philosophical Studies 1. Washington, DC: The Council for Research in Values and Philosophy.
Zimmerman, Armin. 2004. 'Towards a New Christian Sexual Ethics in the Light of HIV/AIDS'. *International Review of Mission* 93 (369): 255–69.

4

Reflections on Reconciliation and *Ubuntu*

R. NEVILLE RICHARDSON

ATTEMPTS TO HEAL the social body of post-apartheid South Africa have taken many forms. There have been major political initiatives at the national level, such as the Reconstruction and Development Programme and the settlement of land claims. At the local level, municipalities have been radically restructured. The single most obvious official attempt at national healing was surely the Truth and Reconciliation Commission (TRC). This chapter examines two of the central moral pillars on which the TRC was based, and upon which hopes for national healing still rest – reconciliation and *ubuntu*.

The final clause of the Interim Constitution of 1993 provides the framework of reference for the quest for national reconciliation:

> This Constitution provides a historic bridge between the past of a deeply divided society characterized by strife, conflict, untold suffering and injustice, and a future founded on the recognition of human rights, democracy and peaceful co-existence and development opportunities for all South Africans irrespective of colour, race, class, belief or sex.
>
> The pursuit of national unity, the well-being of all South African citizens and peace require reconciliation between the people of South Africa and the reconstruction of society... there is a need for understanding but not revenge, a need for reparation but not retaliation, a need for *ubuntu* but not for victimization. (Cochrane, De Gruchy and Martin 1999, 1)

The clause ends by stating that the possibility of amnesty should be offered to perpetrators of certain politically motivated crimes and violations of human rights. This was a last-minute concession, without which the white former leaders of apartheid South Africa would probably have ceased to collaborate. It gave them and their followers a way out of a corner in which they would otherwise have been trapped.

After 1994, the newly elected South African parliament carried out the provisions of the Interim Constitution and, by the end of 1995, passed the Promotion of National Unity and Reconciliation Act, which carried a five-fold mandate: 'to provide a record of gross human rights violations committed by both the upholders of apartheid and the liberation movements between 1 March 1960 . . . and 6 December 1993; to identify the victims; to recommend possible reparations; to process applications for amnesty; and to make recommendations for measures to prevent future gross violations of human rights.'

Much has been written in evaluation of the TRC's work since it presented its main report in October 1998. Opinion is still deeply divided on its achievements and long-term effects. This chapter considers some of the evaluations and looks for prospects of healing the body of the nation.

Ubuntu-based optimism

Personifying the TRC's work and providing much of its underpinning philosophy was its chairperson, Desmond Tutu. His views are unashamedly Christian, which is not surprising from a retired Archbishop. He always saw God's hand at work in the TRC. He evaluates it with a sense of wonder, reminiscent of the Apostle Paul describing his conversion, saying:

> God does have a sense of humor. Who in their right minds could have imagined South Africa to be an example of anything but the most ghastly awfulness, of how *not* to order a nation's race relations and its governance? We South Africans were the unlikeliest lot and that is precisely why God has chosen us. We cannot really claim much credit ourselves for what we have achieved. We were destined for perdition and were picked out for total annihilation. We were a hopeless case if ever there was one. God intends that others might look at us and take courage. God wants to point to us as a possible beacon of hope, a possible paradigm, and to say, 'Look at South

Africa. They had a nightmare called apartheid. It has ended. Northern Ireland (or wherever), your nightmare will end too. They had a problem regarded as intractable. They are resolving it. No problem anywhere can ever again be considered to be intractable. There is hope for you too.' Our experiment is going to succeed because God wants it to succeed, not only for our glory and aggrandizement but for the sake of God's world. God wants to show that there is life after conflict and repression – that because of forgiveness there is a future. (Tutu 1999, 202)

This has more or less become the authorised view of the TRC. Certainly, considering the complexities of South African politics, the depth of bitterness, suspicion and fear, as well as the obstacles, both conceptual and logistical, it is indeed astonishing that anything like the TRC ever happened. Tutu is aware that his concept of the Commission is primarily theological, and not the normal stuff of politics. 'After all,' he says, 'forgiveness, reconciliation, reparation were not the normal currency in political discourse . . . Forgiveness, confession, and reconciliation were far more at home in the religious sphere' (1999, 80–81). Tutu is also aware of the anomaly of his regular prayers during the proceedings of the Commission, and of the purple Archbishop's cassock he sometimes wore. He acknowledges the oddity of his appointment, 'It is interesting that the President appointed an Archbishop as chairperson of the commission and not, for instance, a judge, since we were to some extent a quasi-judicial body' (1999, 80).

Tutu is convinced that the achievements of the TRC are of the greatest national and social value, not only for South Africa, but also as an example and inspiration to other nations with troubled histories. He is also convinced that the single main ingredient that made the achievements of the TRC possible was a uniquely African ingredient – *ubuntu*. He asks, 'What is it that constrained so many to choose to forgive rather than to demand retribution, to be so magnanimous and ready to forgive rather than to wreak revenge?' His answer is *ubuntu*, and he proceeds to offer a full description of this treasured African moral quality:

> *Ubuntu* is very difficult to render into a Western language. It speaks of the very essence of being human. When we want to give high praise to someone we say, '*Yu, u nobuntu*'; 'Hey, so-and-so has *ubuntu*.'

Then you are generous, you are hospitable, you are friendly and caring and compassionate. You share what you have. It is to say, 'My humanity is caught up, is inextricably bound up in yours.' We belong in a bundle of life. We say, 'A person is a person through other persons.' It is not, 'I think therefore I am.' It says rather: 'I am human because I belong, I participate, I share.' A person with *ubuntu* is open and available to others, affirming of others, does not feel threatened that others are able and good, for he or she has a proper self-assurance that comes from knowing that he or she belongs in a greater whole and is diminished, when others are tortured or oppressed, or treated as if they were less than who they are.

Harmony, friendliness, community are great goods. Social harmony is for us the *summum bonum* – the greatest good. Anything that subverts, that undermines this sought-after good, is to be avoided like the plague. Anger, resentment, lust for revenge, even success through aggressive competitiveness, are corrosive of this good. To forgive is not just to be altruistic. It is the best form of self-interest. What dehumanizes you inexorably dehumanizes me. It gives people resilience, enabling them to survive and emerge still human despite all efforts to dehumanize them. (1999, 31–32)

There is no doubt in Tutu's mind of the central moral place of *ubuntu* in the miracle that was the TRC. He is proud of his fellow Africans who demonstrated *ubuntu* during the TRC's proceedings. He is convinced that their display of *ubuntu* made forgiveness and reconciliation possible.

We now turn to three views very different from that of Tutu, all of them from the political left. One of the views is broadly 'Western' and the other two strongly 'Africanist'. None of these views regards the TRC as a miracle. On the contrary, they all highlight its limitations and judge it to have been a mistake. They warn that any glorified view of the Commission's achievements is in fact a misleading and dangerous error.

Questioning reconciliation

Jakes Gerwel believes that the TRC has assumed too grandiose a position in the general assessment of the political settlement in South Africa after apartheid. He disagrees with the view that the TRC introduced a necessary second phase in the reconstruction of South African society, and that the earlier political settlement was little more than a herald of and preparation for the much-needed work of reconciliation. For him, there is a clear separation between the secular political process and the 'spiritual' concept of reconciliation. He leaves his readers in no doubt as to which of the two is the more important in his estimation. He rejects the concept of reconciliation, for he sees it as contributing to 'a discourse of division' (Gerwel 2000, 284). He describes reconciliation's ideal of love in an organisation as large and complex as a modern state as unrealistic and outmoded, an 'idealistic denial or obfuscation of contradiction' (283).

However, in Gerwel's opinion, there is a story that holds the South African nation together. He might call it 'our story'. Others may have difficulty in hearing this unifying story amidst the cacophony of conflicting stories that make up South African history, but Gerwel holds fast to a high view of the political process of national unity. In spite of acknowledging many fault lines, some organic, such as tribal demarcations, some constructed and imposed, such as colonialism and apartheid, he points to a longstanding and overriding political process of national unity. His is an attractive view that merits serious attention. Gerwel claims that, 'there tangibly exists a political basis to a united South African nationhood and that the nation as a political and juridical entity is not threatened by disintegration or social disruption' (2000, 282).

His purpose is to demystify the view that the transition from racial minority rule to non-racial democracy was miraculous. He holds up the secular political process, rather than 'the current, more spiritual notion of reconciliation', which operates 'primarily amongst individuals or sets of individual actors' (2000, 279). As a vehicle for national reconciliation, the TRC is not seen as worthless per se, but the limits of its usefulness within the context of a secular national structure are driven home. More substantial claims for the TRC's value are decisively rejected:

> The TRC constituted an important moment in the transitionary process – within which deeply human, subjective forces were allowed to attain precedence over the objective forces of state politics. The extent to which the tensions and inevitable pain associated with remembering the past were accentuated, should not be allowed to distract from the remarkable progress the nation

has already made on the journey of political coexistence. The appeal is that we do not pathologize a nation in relatively good health by demanding a perpetual quest for the Holy Grail of reconciliation. (Gerwel 2000, 286)

Gerwel therefore makes a clear distinction between reconciliation and national unity, and offers a necessary and honest evaluation of the TRC. His argument is partly historical. He points to significant features in the secular political process, at least from the time of the Union of South Africa in 1910, which he regards as key ingredients for eventual unity among the various social groups in South Africa. Seen in this light, the Constitution of 1996 is not an entirely new legal phenomenon, but rather the high point of a long process. As Gerwel states:

> It is important to recognize the 1996 Constitution as not only a founding pact, and hence starting point, but equally importantly as the culmination of a long process of resistance against segregation and apartheid, in defence of the unity of the post-1910 South African nation. This recognition provides a valuable qualification to the approach emphasizing the novelty of the nation and its challenges of reconciliation. (2000, 282)

He points out that the mainstream of the liberation struggle was inspired by the vision of non-racial unity in the nation. He puts the TRC squarely in a subservient place, with the firm reminder that it owes its very existence to a political agreement and mandate. Certainly the provision that gave birth to the TRC is enshrined in a key statement of the 1993 Interim Constitution: 'The pursuit of national unity, the well-being of all South African citizens and peace require reconciliation between the people of South Africa and the reconstruction of society' (Cochrane, De Gruchy and Martin 1999, 1).

It is significant that the part played by the institutional churches in the proceedings of the TRC was so small as to be described as follows: 'Given the scope of the TRC's mandate, the faith community hearings were but a small dab on a much larger canvas' (Cochrane, De Gruchy and Martin 1999, 5). Extending the metaphor, it could be said that in Gerwel's estimation, the TRC itself is but a small spiritual dab on the much larger canvas of political progress towards national unity. It must now be asked what positive prospects for reconciliation, peace and social healing in South Africa are offered in Gerwel's admirable analysis.

Gerwel offers a democratic process based on a theory of social contract. Citizens are to rally around the political arrangements that lead to national unity, and to agree on ways to restrain any possibilities of racial injustice arising again. That, surely, is desirable in comparison with the social and political arrangement that preceded it, an arrangement fittingly described by Tutu as 'the most ghastly awfulness' (1999, 282).

Three questions, however, must be asked of Gerwel. First, can he conceive of a community with peace as its supreme common good, given that his underlying political philosophy seems firmly grounded in the Enlightenment with its ingrained individualism? Second, can Gerwel's thinking sustain a concept of peace that is any more than the absence of conflict? Third, his argument assumes a dualistic separation of the political process from religious influences. Does this dualistic structure of his thought not result in the relegation of religious faith to such an indirect and minimal role in the political process that its community-creating power is shrivelled to insignificance?

On the first two points, it is difficult to see how Gerwel can free himself, even if he wanted to, from the limits of a Hobbesian-type social contract. Does he envisage a community rooted in anything more than negotiation and political compromise? How would he describe a peace that is more than the absence of conflict? Surely South Africa needs more than that. Its story of oppression, deprivation, pain, alienation, fragmentation and struggle needs to be superseded by a new story of social wholeness and constructive peace. Such a desirable state of affairs, it seems, needs to be comprised of more than political settlement and national unity alone. There is a past that needs forgiving, however minimal a place Gerwel would grant such a 'subjective' consideration. There is also a future that needs envisioning, a future that includes necessary goods other than social reconciliation and economic justice. Where is such a vision to be imagined and how are people to be formed with the moral character and social skills necessary for the vision to be realised in communal form? Who will be the architects and artisans of its construction? By drawing a decisive sacred-secular divide, and then setting both his feet firmly on the secular side, it seems that Gerwel deprives himself of essential wellsprings of human vision and virtue. The necessary ingredients of moral vision, character-building and community development seem to be missing, as they are in so much political and social-ethical thinking that has been inspired and shaped, yet limited, by the Enlightenment. For Gerwel, the contribution of the TRC may best be in its role as an agency of memory and the production of national narratives:

> It is in the construction of such a lineage of narratives of national remembrance that the TRC may be found to have made its most lasting contribution. As an event of story-telling, confession and forgiving, within a quasi-judicial framework, it represented a unique moment in the country's history – an interstitial pause for a nation to acknowledge its unity and intimate inter-connections also in perversity and suffering. (Gerwel 2000, 280)

This route to national unity by way of memory and narrative sounds attractive and plausible. In stating its importance, it is almost as if Gerwel gives back to the TRC some of the importance he has denied it. But why should such narratives be unifying, rather than divisive? For it is often in clinging to group narratives, especially those of 'perversity and suffering' that the worst inter-group violence is generated. The conflict in South Africa's apartheid society was, to a large extent, a rallying around and giving of political expression to conflicting group narratives.

Essential for reconciliation, peace and social healing are narratives sufficient to convey the truth of the past, especially the painful, even the guilt-ridden episodes that are conveniently forgotten, which are capable of either bonding people together or driving them apart, depending on how they are treated. The difficulty lies in the fact that such narratives do not float in the air. They are preserved in and carried by particular communities. There is a necessary dialectical connection between narrative and community – each requires the other for its existence. Narrative needs community if it is to last across generations, and community needs narrative if it is to have a sense of its own identity and its distinction from other communities. Yet it is often the very communities that have the most developed narratives and sense of identity that are most hostile towards other communities. As well as in South Africa, examples of such self-centred and hostile communities may be found in many other troubled parts of the world –

Israel-Palestine, Northern Ireland, Rwanda, Bosnia and Croatia. How does Gerwel propose that the production of narratives per se will unify the nation and reconcile its communities?

Gerwel is surely correct in acknowledging the vital social importance of narratives, but which narratives in particular does he have in mind? Will those narratives, while being truthful, also be healing and reconciling, rather than more divisive? Nothing in the structure of his thought shows why the narratives should be of one kind, rather than another. The structure of his thought also does not allow for particular communities of the kind that can embody and generate healing and reconciliation. Structurally, he recognizes two levels of relationship. There are individual relationships, of the kind that the TRC engages. By contrast, there are complex societal relationships of an impersonal kind, mediated through political processes. Do his envisaged narratives somehow hold together the personal and the political spheres? How, in this typically Enlightenment way of thinking, can there be narratives of healing and reconciliation, and communities of reconciliation and healing? Gerwel's analysis leaves these vital questions unanswered.

'Dealing lightly with the wound of my people'

A second view deeply critical of the TRC is that of Tinyiko Maluleke. His diagnosis is that the TRC has dealt superficially with what he calls 'the deep and glaring wound of South African people' and therefore has not effected healing (Maluleke 1997, 324). He reinforces his diagnosis by characterising the greater response of black people as 'absence and silence' (1999, 101–13). One reason for his jeremiad is that the victims who submitted their grievances, some of whom testified before the Commission, received no reparation for their suffering and loss. It goes without saying that at the least, he would want there to be reparations of a kind that make demands on the perpetrators. With many others, he rightly sees it as anomalous that a perpetrator whose awful deeds bolstered apartheid, could receive almost instant amnesty and walk free to enjoy the benefits that apartheid bestowed on him, while his victim remains sunk in misery and deprivation.

More fundamental to Maluleke's diagnosis is a conceptual concern. He argues that the Commission has monopolised the meaning of the term 'reconciliation' and has cast it in a liberal-individualist mould. Thus conceived, the term is virtually restricted in its application to acts of atrocity.

It loses sight of the massive ongoing structural atrocity, the 'legalized crime' in Maluleke's words, that was apartheid in all its ramifications. He argues that 'apart from minimizing the role of systems and institutions in the apartheid crime against humanity, this approach also reduces the apartheid evil to the acts of its worst perpetrators as well as forcing an artificial "equality" between beneficiaries and the victimized' (Maluleke 1999, 110).

The profundity of this evil lay in its everyday, commonplace presence, a presence, which restricted, disadvantaged, and oppressed black South Africans in almost every aspect of life. Maluleke is surely correct in his view that the profound evil of apartheid and its ongoing effects in the present and the future will not be healed by a 'small, temporary and extremely limited commission', which considers the cases of merely a few thousand victims and perpetrators (1997, 324). This is a wound that affects the vast majority in a population of over forty million, and in its social, economic and psychological effects also spans generations.

Even if the life of the TRC were to have been extended indefinitely and its resources expanded vastly, Maluleke does not think that its concepts and methods could ever have effected healing. In this view, Maluleke follows the incisive critique of Mahmood Mamdani, whose chief complaint is aimed at the TRC's blurring of the boundary between the political, the moral, and the truthful. The desired political compromise has been transfigured into a moral virtue. Mamdani says: 'I am not opposed to the compromise . . . I am not opposed to the amnesty. What I am opposed to is turning the political compromise into a moral one, letting it become the boundary of truth telling' (cited in Maluleke 1999, 109).

For Maluleke, herein lies the negative effect of the TRC concept and process: '[The TRC] stifles the social debate in the name of maintaining social peace. In the name of maintaining social peace it turns the political boundaries of a compromise into analytical boundaries of truth seeking, and by reinforcing the political compromise with a compromised truth it turns the political compromise into a moral compromise' (Maluleke 1997, 109).

Maluleke hears the offered rebuttal that the TRC was a limited instrument – it was limited in the terms of reference of its mandate, in its resources and in the time allocated to it (1999, 105). Mamdani's devastating critique, however, leads Maluleke to appeal for the maintenance of 'a strict distinction between the TRC as an inadequate instrument on the one hand and the ideal of reconciliation and truth-telling on the other' (1999, 113). Mamdani is prepared to entertain the idea of 'a different commission' that will 'bring to light the truth the TRC has obscured; a commission which would put centre-stage the experience of apartheid as a banal reality'(Mamdani cited in Maluleke, 1999, 110). Such a Commission would have been very different, in that it would have had vastly increased legal and political powers. Its investigations could then give rise to a new, more truthful, and more morally adequate social debate. Maluleke is more pessimistic than Mamdani on this point. He decisively rejects the TRC with its 'severely limited understanding of justice borne out of a political compromise' (1999, 111).

For Maluleke, the TRC was based on and proceeded according to a flawed understanding in respect of truth, reconciliation and justice. As a result, it has left the impression that social healing, or at least a major step in that direction has taken place, whereas it has not. Indeed, the vast majority of the victims of apartheid has been marginalised and has not been heard. Their wounds remain unattended. Their 'absence and silence' (Maluleke 1999, 101–13) is eloquent, and must be considered with the utmost seriousness.

Gerwel's critique points to a demystified account of and a minimised role for reconciliation, and holds up an objective, secular political process conducive of national unity. He seems quite optimistic as to the long-term likelihood of the success of this process. Maluleke's more pessimistic critique reminds us of the profound depths of the apartheid evil, and emphasises that that such evil cannot be healed by a limited device called 'reconciliation' between some victims and some perpetrators, such as that offered by the TRC. Both views point to the deleterious effects of confusing the TRC's work with the great social healing that is so badly needed. When a proper distinction is not maintained, the TRC's work, now complete, encourages a false belief that the business of truth-telling is now over, that reconciliation has been effected, and that South African society is healed. Such a view would be mistaken indeed.

As with Gerwel, Maluleke seems to be correct in his diagnosis, but what is his proposed cure? It is all very well to point out the inadequacies of a brave attempt at healing such as the TRC. Such a pessimistic diagnosis might be understandable from a social critic especially, as in this case, from an incisive black social critic, but it is not enough for a response that declares itself to be theological. It is important at this point to note that, while

Gerwel makes no such claim, Maluleke explicitly claims his analysis to be theological. What then does he see as the outcome of the TRC's failure to heal? His dire warning echoes the prophets of the Old Testament: 'Black people will rise up against the powers that be, though all indications are that this will happen only after the time of "our father" and "our uncle".' The father and uncle, rather disparagingly referred to, are, of course, Mandela and Tutu respectively. Precisely who will rise up now that political power is in black hands? Probably those whom Maluleke regards as being silent and absent from the TRC discourse, 'black women, the poor and the marginalized' (Maluleke 1999, 104). Against whom will these people rise up? Will it be those white people who are still in power positions of various kinds, economic power perhaps? Or will it be against the newly powerful and rich – the rapidly emergent black ruling elite?

While one can support Maluleke's general diagnosis of the inadequacies of the TRC, it must be pointed out that the mandate of the TRC was never to redress the vast structural problems and economic disparities of South Africa. It will take decades of good governance to address that, rather than the three-year life span and limited resources of a small commission. As for individual perpetrators contributing to their victims in the form of 'guilt tax' or reparation, while this would seem perfectly just, and a small price to pay for release from the criminal weight of their past, such a prospect would, in all probability, have scared off the confessors. They would then have been more inclined to take their chances in court, where lack of evidence may well have had an amnesty-like effect. And, after all, the TRC was about getting at truth rather than recompense, restorative justice, rather than punitive justice.

Was the TRC a miracle or a mistake? The commissioners themselves would be the first to admit the limitations and flaws in the work of the Commission and its outcomes. But with them, I would point to the gains and suggest that South Africa with the limited, circumscribed chemotherapy of the TRC is better off than if the many cancers of apartheid had been left entirely untreated. I must agree with both Gerwel and Maluleke, however, that reflection on the TRC holds out a temptation of imagining it to have been much more of a full healing process than it was or ever could be. To succumb to this temptation would be to be guilty of a theology of 'cheap grace', as Maluleke points out (1997, 326). Apart from his negative critique, however, what does Maluleke's theology bring to the struggle for reconciliation, peace and social healing?

Maluleke's response is profoundly negative. In his estimation, the TRC has not effected social healing. In fact, it has done damage to the meaning of the term 'reconciliation' by its focus on atrocities, rather than on apartheid in its awful entirety, and it has silenced the voice of the poor black masses. In his view, the TRC has given the impression of having satisfied the demands of truth and reconciliation, whereas, in fact, it has achieved little more than a political compromise. As for social healing, Maluleke invokes theology, but the substance of his theology is unclear. He closes his evaluation of the TRC by pointing in the direction of black theology: 'The prospects for black theological reflection on truth and reconciliation discourse are vast and varied. I suggest that black absence-silence is the crucial point of departure for such reflection. Furthermore, black theology has at least four decades of discussion and reflections on reconciliation to build on' (1999, 113). Unfortunately this pointer does not help us to take even the first step on the journey towards reconciliation and healing.

A more recent article shows a remarkable development in Maluleke's thinking on many aspects of social reconciliation. He still feels that 'the work of reconciliation and reparation was barely begun by the TRC process' (2005, 113), but his main terms of reference seem to have undergone a transformation. Instead of vast prospects for black theological reflection, he now sees, almost with reluctance and disbelief, that his previously held theological perspectives have had their day. 'Could it be that the neat and established Liberation Theology, Black Consciousness, ANC-struggle rhetoric about reconciliation and even about truth had reached its limits? My observations slowly convinced me that the reconciliation discourse had entered a different level. It was still precarious and very untidy, but it was of a different order than my inherited traditions allowed for' (Maluleke 2005, 111).

There is a striking shift to a far more positive attitude regarding the whole work of reconciliation in South Africa. In this later view, Maluleke is no longer disparaging of the reconciling work of Mandela and Tutu. So positive is his view of Mandela that he now credits Mandela's 'visionary leadership' with the achievement of a 'bridge between the past and the future' that formed part of the initial political inspiration for the Commission

(2005, 111). Far from his previous emphatic envisaging of a revolutionary uprising of black people after the time of Mandela and Tutu, Maluleke is now much more hopeful. While still struggling with the painful memories of the past he declares: 'Over the past decade my faith in the future of myself and my children in this country has been restored' (2005, 119). Clearly Maluleke has come to a point where he thinks the process of social reconciliation is well under way.

The manipulation of *ubuntu*

Although Wim van Binsbergen hails from Holland, his sociological and anthropological studies have focused on Africa since the early 1970s. He has studied African society and has identified with it to the extent that he describes himself not only as 'an analyst and a participant', but also as 'an honorary African' who enjoys 'the status of diviner-priest' (Van Binsbergen 2002).

His careful study of the term *ubuntu* acknowledges its widespread use today. Not only does it occur in everyday speech, but also in the most sophisticated contexts, and 'as a concept in management ideologies in the transitional stages of post-apartheid'. Van Binsbergen says:

> In the hands of academic philosophers, *ubuntu/hunhu* has become a key concept to evoke the unadulterated forms of African social life before the European conquest. The world-view (in other words the values, beliefs and images) of pre-colonial Southern Africa is claimed to survive today, more or less, in remote villages and intimate kin relationships, and to constitute an inspiring blue-print for the present and future of social, economic and political life in urban and modern environments, at the very centres of the economy and the political system (2002).

He argues that, in spite of the apparent transparency of *ubuntu*, its meaning cannot be precisely rendered. Referring to the speech-act categories of J.L. Austin, he argues that any factual (locutionary) use, or even assumed meaning (illocutionary) cannot be substantiated, because the use of *ubuntu* is persuasive (perlocutionary). Speaking of *ubuntu* and similar terms, he claims that it is easy to see that they are not factual descriptions. The communities that are assumed to have embodied them are no longer to be found and, ironically, in those communities, the term *ubuntu* seems not to have been used. Even traditional and rural communities in Africa today are tainted with the effects of colonialism and globalisation. What then, according to Van Binsbergen, is the function of the term *ubuntu* and similar terms today?

> They primarily express the speaker's dreams about norms and practices that allegedly once prevailed in what are now to be considered *peripheral* places (notably within the intimacy of allegedly closely-knit villages, urban wards and kin groups), while the speaker himself or herself is situated at or near the national or global centre. Such dreams about the past and periphery are articulated, not because the speaker proposes to retire there personally or wishes to exhort other people to take up effective residence there, but because of their inspiring modelling power with regard to the central national and even global issues – in other words, because of these dreams' alleged persuasive/perlocutionary nature outside the peripheral domain in which they are claimed to originate and to which they refer back. (2002)

Unlike some commentators who regard *ubuntu* as a hedge against the encroachment of globalisation on Africa, Van Binsbergen regards *ubuntu* itself to be the product of globalisation. This is partly as a result of the dominance of North Atlantic forms of expression and argument which decree that our constructions, however African we may want them to be, 'need to be formulated in the academic and commodified format stipulated (even imposed) by the North Atlantic hegemony' (Van Binsbergen 2002). A common method of de-emphasising the North Atlantic nature of our thinking, he says, is to call this process 'global' or 'universal'. He then proceeds to note the contradictions in everyday life to which this strange function of the term *ubuntu* gives rise, such as the living of 'a double life' by so many modern urban Africans. The point to which Van Binsbergen is leading is that the term *ubuntu* should not be used naively and that its uninformed use can lead to serious difficulties.

> If *ubuntu* is to be Africa's great gift to the global world of thought, it is primarily not the African villager's gift, but that of the academic

and managerial codifiers who allowed themselves to be distantly and selectively inspired by village life: ignoring the ubiquitous conflicts and contradictions, the oppressive immanence of the world-view, the witchcraft beliefs and accusations the constant oscillations between trust and distrust, and merely appropriating the bright side. (2002)

Therefore, an informed use of the term *ubuntu*, according to Van Binsbergen, recognises its persuasive power and its prophetic and utopian functions. With the cautions that he provides, he believes that *ubuntu*, like many other African concepts, can help place African and therefore different elements into the global scene. More especially, it can be useful 'in the creation of a moral community of people concerned about the present and future of Southern Africa, which ... I identified as the obvious goal of the *ubuntu* philosophy'. In the face of intolerable and insurmountable contradictions such as those faced by the TRC, an appeal to *ubuntu* has the potential to act as 'a lubricant of social relations'. It 'produces sociability and alleviates tensions' (2002).

The great danger that Van Binsbergen wants to expose is that such beneficial effects of *ubuntu* should not be assumed to make real conflicts disappear. It is at this point that he launches into his withering criticism of the TRC and its public co-option of the concept of *ubuntu*. His concern is that the central concept of reconciliation at the heart of the TRC was fundamentally and exclusively Christian: 'It can be no accident that no traditional diviner-priests (guardians of the ancestral world-view) participated in the TRC context, where they could have articulated Southern African viewpoints on evil, sin and not only the possibility, but also the limitations of expiation' (2002). In the absence of such experts, he argues, it was the concept of *ubuntu* alone that had to function as the bridge for bringing traditional guidance into those emotionally fraught deliberations. This had the effect of skewing the moral playing field.

> The black African population of South Africa, having been immensely wronged by the White people with a European background, was in the end not even free to define the terms under which it would be prepared to leave this past behind them, and to include regional historical elements of an African culture of justice

and expiation among these terms; no, even the terms of reconciliation were set by European and White dominance – even if this dominance had the amicable, integrity-exuding and unmistakably Black face of Archbishop Tutu. The TRC and the occasional appeal to *ubuntu* in that connection, conveyed the suggestion that unconditional forgiveness and cleansing merely on the basis of a verbal admission of guilt is part of the Southern African ancestral heritage. Such a suggestion is misleading... The perpetrators of atrocities under the apartheid state qualify as sorcerers and might have been treated accordingly. For such treatment a number of more or less draconian precepts are available. This is one major example of how under contemporary conditions *ubuntu* is pressed into service at the centre of national political affairs, in mystifying ways that deny or pervert time-honoured African values, under the pretence of articulating those very values. (Van Binsbergen 2002)

Then follows a chilling and prophetic sentence that closely echoes the warning of Maluleke in his earlier, pessimistic mode: 'In years to come South African society will yet have to pay the price for the massive and manipulative repression of resentment and anger caused by the historically ungrounded use of *ubuntu* in the context of the TRC' (2002).

Unlike Maluleke who leaves it unclear as to whom the anger will be directed against, Van Binsbergen follows this warning with a further example of the misuse of *ubuntu*, this time pointing to the increasing class conflict in southern Africa. He sees the newly privileged using *ubuntu* 'as a mystifying concept' to justify their crossing over 'to the privileged side of the huge class divide, without being over-sensitive to the wider social costs of their individual economic and status advancement' (2002).

Van Binsbergen's fear is that through misuse the liberative term *ubuntu* carries the seeds of its own opposite or denial. In the past, other words describing the 'peoplehood' of Africans, such as *bantu*, have been manipulated to become expressions of Black exclusion and oppression. His positive proposal is that through awareness of the complexities and contradictions of *ubuntu*, and alertness to its manipulation and misuse, the term and concept will indeed point to the Arcadian vision of Africanness, and thereby be instrumental in the social progression towards the utopia of moral community.

Conclusion: A social vision

Both reconciliation and *ubuntu* have played significant roles in the development of the new South African society, but those roles are not as romantic and unproblematic as is often assumed. Reconciliation has its roots in Christian faith. *Ubuntu* has its roots in African tradition. Both have their proper place and meaning in respect of particular communities. Like other moral concepts, they are community-referential and arguably, have little clarity or usefulness as universal, abstract concepts. Such ill-advised usage may well, as noted above, result in their co-option for profitable use by those with ulterior motives. From the discussion above, it would appear that both terms have been used in the context of post-apartheid South Africa in an abstract and universal sense and, as such, have been open to manipulation and abuse, even to the extent of becoming subtle tools of a new oppression.

It is clear that the original historical societies from which the terms are assumed to have sprung are no longer accessible to the people of the modern world, either experientially or conceptually. Just as the gulf has been pointed out between modern and traditional African societies, so the small, intimate house church in a first-century Greek seaport, to which the New Testament concept of reconciliation initially applied, is out of reach to us. Ours is a modern, scientific, global society, and we are shaped, for better or for worse, by the forces known as 'globalisation'. Yet it is surely possible for us to approximate, faithfully and creatively, a social and economic matrix that embodies reconciliation and that embodies *ubuntu*. Our morality today desperately needs such social guidance. This is not an appeal for us to become Arcadian, to try to reconstruct the past and live in it. Rather, this is written in the hope that we may be open to the vision of what our present and future society might be when inspired by what was best (and warned by what was worst) in the past. It is written in the hope that our moral concepts will be faithfully and honestly shaped with our social realities in mind, and that our future social and economic realities, in turn, will become the embodiments of the best in our vision of the past.

Select bibliography

Cochrane, J., J. de Gruchy and S. Martin (eds.). 1999. *Facing the Truth: South African Faith Communities and the Truth and Reconciliation Commission*. Cape Town: David Philip.

Gerwel, Jakes. 2000. 'National Reconciliation: Holy Grail or Secular Pact?'. In *Looking Back, Reaching Forward: Reflections on the Truth and Reconciliation Commission of South Africa*, eds. Charles Villa-Vicencio and Wilhelm Verwoerd, 277–86. Cape Town: University of Cape Town Press and London: Zed Books.

Maluleke, Tinyiko S. 1997. '"Dealing Lightly with the Wound of My People"? The TRC Process in Theological Perspective'. *Missionalia* 25 (3) (November): 324–43.

———. 1999. 'The Truth and Reconciliation Discourse: A Black Theological Evaluation'. In *Facing the Truth: South African Faith Communities and the Truth and Reconciliation Commission*, eds. J. Cochrane, J. de Gruchy and S. Martin, 101–13. Cape Town: David Philip.

———. 2005. 'Reconciliation in South Africa: Ten Years Later'. *Journal of Theology for Southern Africa* 123 (November): 105–20.

Ramose, Mogobe B. 2002. 'The Philosophy of *Ubuntu* and *Ubuntu* as Philosophy'. In *Philosophy From Africa*, 2nd edition, eds. P.H. Coetzee and A.P.J. Roux, 230–38. Oxford: Oxford University Press.

Tutu, Desmond Mpilo. 1999. *No Future Without Forgiveness*. New York: Doubleday.

Van Binsbergen, Wim. 2002. 'Ubuntu and the Globalisation of Southern African Thought and Society'. http://www.shikanda.net/general/ubuntu.htm (accessed 15 August 2004).

5

On African Ethics and the Appropriation of Western Capitalism

Cultural and Moral Constraints to the Evolution of Capitalism in Post-colonial Africa

MUNYARADZI FELIX MUROVE

IN 1993 MY FRIEND invited me to accompany him on a courtesy visit to his relatives who stayed in a rural area called Murewa, 40 kilometres from Harare, the capital city of Zimbabwe. Although nobody knew that we were coming, we were met with great jubilation on our arrival. Neighbours came to greet us, asking us whether everything was well where we came from and within a short period of time, we were given some roasted groundnuts to eat, while dinner was being prepared. A live sheep was presented to us according to custom. After we clapped our hands in gratitude, the sheep was taken away for slaughter.

While this was happening, some neighbourhood children were sent to the shopping centre to buy drinks for us. We offered to pay, but the father of the family reminded us that we were visiting them. In their culture, part of what it means to be human is that his family was obliged to provide for us in whatever way they could. The mother of the family said jokingly, 'We are not like you town people who always expect those who visit you to bring their own food.' Everybody laughed. However, she continued to ask my friend, 'When are you coming back home? It is not good to stay in town. Town life breeds an erosion of character.' My friend answered that he had bought a house in town. Everybody looked at him with a sense of surprise and confusion. Her reply was that Harare was not home, but only a place of work.

Even though this family was poor, their generosity, sense of humour, laughter and their fervent keenness to know our well-being left me tongue-tied. After dinner we gave them some groceries that we had bought for them as gifts, which they received with great ululation and dancing. Before we went to bed, we told them of our intention to leave the following morning, but they insisted that we should stay for another day or two. Clearly they did not worry about the costs that they were going to incur; their main concern was our being together.

Introduction

The experience described above led me to the idea that the African economic context has two economic systems that seem to exist side by side. We have a modern economic system that is urban and another that is rural or traditional. The modern economy is Western-orientated, while the rural economy works according to African traditional values. Although Western capitalism has been in Africa for a long time, these dual economies have remained separate.

The collapse of Communism more than a decade ago has meant that advocates of neo-liberal capitalism see Western capitalism as the only remaining economic system applicable to all humanity today. However, the triumph of Western capitalism has carried with it rapid economic decay in many African countries. The economic mentoring that has been offered to African countries by the IMF and the World Bank has proved futile in many African states because after the economic mentoring sessions, the economic condition of these African states has deteriorated from bad to worse.

Despite the fact that our institutions of higher learning have remained dedicated to the teaching of economics and business studies under the paradigm of Western patterns of economic thought, in practice such academic endeavours have not resulted in the appropriation of Western capitalism in post-colonial Africa. While a small percentage of the African population purports to live under the value systems of Western capitalism, many people still feel that where they belong is in the traditional communal setting that is mostly dominated by traditional values. Within this African traditional setting, land is owned in common and private property is also subject to common use. The traditional African economic world remains foreign to the other small, Westernised, urban economy. These two worlds have remained separate because their values are not compatible: the emphasis on community that has dominated traditional community-based economic relations is contradictory to modern economic relations built on Western individualistic values.

Whilst African traditional economic relations emphasise communal well-being and individual belonging, economic relations that are based on Western capitalism emphasise individual autonomy, the individual pursuit for personal gain and the primacy of rational choice. African communitarian values are making it impossible for modern capitalism to be integrated into traditional African life. Modern ways of doing business, such as banking and the credit card system, do not exist in the African traditional economic setting. Documentation of properties so as to designate private ownership, as is the main practice of Western capitalism, is also non-existent.

While it has been claimed that Western capitalism is the only viable economic system for socio-economic progress and prosperity, such a claim overlooks the fact that there are certain cultural values that are inherently incompatible with the rationale of Western capitalism. In a cultural context with values based on communal solidarity and human relationality, the Western capitalistic values of individualism and pursuit of profit cannot cohere. If cultural values pose a limit to the appropriation of Western capitalism in post-colonial Africa, I would like to argue that an understanding of African economic relations emphasise African cultural values, rather than being exclusively concerned with imposing Western capitalistic practices on African economic relations. This chapter is a work of advocacy in the sense that I am advocating the idea that Africa has its own cultural values that have inhibited the appropriation of Western capitalism.

The colonial heritage and the appropriation of Western capitalism
Post-colonial African scholars argue that Western capitalism was introduced to the Africans in ways that were contrary to African traditional values such as respect, a sense of caring for others and a concern for the well-being of others. Colonialism is seen as an historical epoch characterised by greed and the exploitation of Africans (Vambe 1972, 95; see also Gross 1956). However, the mediation of Western capitalism into Africa through colonialism also carried with it a twisting of the values that were usually associated with classic Western capitalism. Ali Mazrui argues that this

twisting of Western capitalistic values can be traced to the way in which capitalism historically arrived in Africa:

> Capitalism arrived in Africa with the imperative of acquisition without the discipline of work and frugality. The white man himself in Africa set a dangerous example. He never washed his own clothes, or cooked his own food, or polished his own shoes, or made his own bed, or cleaned his own room, or even poured his own gin and tonic. [This] luxurious life ... was detrimental to the spirit of capitalism the white man himself had arrived with. Africa's own prestige motive – which had been sociable in its original versions – now was transformed by the aristocratic life-style imported by the white man. (Mazrui 1990, 493)

Thus one of the reasons for the failure of Western capitalism in Africa can be traced to the fact that the colonial interface introduced this peculiar work ethic that was alien to Western capitalism itself. The theory of economic development through hard work and frugality that was advanced by the sociologist Max Weber as the main cause of the rise of modern Western capitalism was reversed.

The idea of labour in colonial Africa was inseparably associated with slavery. Colonial historian, Hamilton Johnston, writes:

> The negro, more than any other human type, has been marked by his mental and physical characteristics as the servant of other races ... In his primitive state he is born a slave. He is possessed of great physical strength, docility, cheerfulness of disposition, a short memory for sorrows and cruelties ... Above all, he can toil hard under the sun and in the unhealthy climates of the torrid zone. (1913, 151)

Within such writing, it is evident that the colonial ethic of work accorded superiority to the laziness of white people. The legacy of this work ethic in post-colonial Africa can be seen especially in those instances when it has become customary to hear people talking about 'the workers' as only referring to Africans. It is common knowledge that white people are seen as hording the money while others work – hence the word '*umulungu*' is used to refer to someone who has money, be they black or white.

However, documents on pre-colonial African economic relations provide evidence that Western capitalism and African traditional ethics have quite different attitudes to labour. A Portuguese trader diarised the following:

> When the Portuguese found themselves in the land of gold [Manyika] they thought they would immediately be able to fill sacks with it and carry off as much as they chose; but when they spend a few days near the mines, and saw the difficulty and labour of the Kiffirs [*sic*], and with what risk and peril to their lives they extracted it from the bowels of the earth and from the stones, they found their hopes frustrated. (cited in Mudenge 1988, 176)

In the same vein, a Father Monclaro wrote that when Munhumutapa gave the Portuguese gold mines, 'they would not accept it in as much as there is greater expenditure in extracting the gold, and but little in a day; business and trade are more profitable' (cited in Mudenge 1988, 176). However, the ethic of hard work was more highly valued in pre-colonial Africa than itinerary trade.

There seems to have been a conviction among Africans that labour had more value than its product. The idea of assigning more value to the product and less to the labour that produced it would thus have been shocking within the pre-colonial African context. In African traditional ethics, labour did not have greater productivity than its *telos*. Rather, the goal was to enhance individual well-being through communal participation. Labour done together encapsulated aesthetic values because it was integral to the practical articulation of what it means to be human and to belong to the community (Marquard and Standing 1939, 20–32; Samkange and Samkange 1980, 80–81). In an atmosphere of enjoyment with others, labour was conceptualised as something pleasurable, rather than something to be endured. With the advent of Western capitalism through colonialism, the idea of labour was severed from its communal aesthetic orientation to a functional understanding of a human being as a labour machine. People then experienced themselves as valued purely on the basis of what they could produce – a total contrast to their traditional concept of labour. As Benezet Bujo puts it:

> Work was, so to say, part of the human being. It helped to intensify the life force of the community... It is a well-known fact that in traditional Africa, work had nothing to do with 'salary'. The development of the clan's community life is what was emphasized. In other words: work was seen in its humanizing dimension. It did not merely exist for the sake of getting rich. (1998, 163–64)

African traditional society understood labour as an expression of one's humanness, which was an articulation of solidarity with the community. Such an understanding of labour served moral purposes that had nothing to do with the Western capitalistic conceptualisation of work that is wholly dominated by a profit motive. Within African traditional society, communal solidarity through labour called forth the full participation of all members of society – hence singing, dancing, and drinking of alcohol during labour was integral to the celebration of the liveliness of the community. Marie and Stanlake Samkange argue that contrary to the African humanistic conceptualisation of work, when Western capitalistic labour was introduced to the Africans through colonialism, its introduction was accompanied by crude dehumanisation: 'Here, at work or in the *komboni*, the motto was: "*Mugwazo*" (Finish your piece of work) "*Indoda iya zibonela*" (Each one for himself). There was no spirit of working together' (Samkange and Samkange 1980, 87). The implication of this observation is that African traditional values that were associated with labour have never been integrated into Western capitalistic work practices.

The African prestige motive and the appropriation of Western capitalism

Mazrui argues that Western capitalism could not adapt itself properly in the African context because the prestige motive (rather than the profit motive) is more prominent in African economic relations. This prestige motive arises from the African fear of being rejected or disapproved of by the community (Mazrui 1966, 137–38). Instead of the profit motive, the prestige motive arises from the individual's need for communal belonging:

> The fear of social disapproval in traditional societies is the minimal impulse in the individual. At a certain stage of expansion that fear becomes something more positive – the desire of prestige. This

prestige motive arises out of the collectivistic sensitivities of individuals in traditional societies . . . Desire for prestige within the traditional unit is therefore often stronger impulse than any individualistic profit motive of the Western type. (138)

Obviously the prestige motive would be incompatible with the orthodox principle of Western capitalism that says that the individual should always relate to and co-operate with the community only after calculating the costs and benefits to be accrued from such co-operation. The ascendancy of Western capitalism inhibited those African moral values that emphasise concern for the community above personal gain.

The evolution of Western capitalism went hand in hand with scholarly condemnation of the prestige motive in matters pertaining to economic relations. In the seventeenth century, Dutch physician Bernard Mandeville wrote a parody called *The Fable of the Bees*, in which he argued that public benefits were the outcomes of private vices and not of private virtues. His conviction was that the economic affairs of the world were not based on the subjugation of passions and vices but on 'pride, vanity, and self-love'. If these qualities were to be denied, then society would be reduced to a state of unprecedented gruesome misery and poverty (Mandeville 1924, 267–71; see also Lux 1990, 116–19).

Mandeville argues that if all actions were to cease except those that arise from the prestige motive, trade would end, the arts would be unnecessary and crafts would be abandoned. Thus he poetised his imagined economic tragedy as follows:

As Pride and Luxury decrease,
So by degrees they leave the Seas.
Not Merchants now, but Companies
Remove whole Manufactories
. . . So few in the vast Hive remain
The hundredth Party they can't maintain. (1924, 34–35)

According to Mandeville, the introduction of virtue or the prestige motive in a society that was thriving on vices led to the ruining of a prosperous hive or the economy. His argument in the stanza above is that if vices, luxury and corruption are connected with economic prosperity, then virtue will only lead to economic decay and poverty. Vices of the individual in the profit motive may be private, but they are public virtues because they benefit society in the long run (Mandeville 1924, 36–37; see also Goldsmith 1985, 34–35; Radcliffe 1994, 762–63). Thus in the evolution of Western capitalism, the profit motive became the sole determinant of human economic relations and motivation. The father of Western capitalism, Adam Smith, echoed Mandeville's parody and taught that '[t]he economic agent intends only his own gain', but in the process, '[b]y pursuing his own interest he frequently promotes that of the society more effectually than when he really intends to promote it' (1976, 423). Thus Smith reduced human economic motives to the pursuit of personal gain. The gains that society at large might derive from the individual's pursuit of personal gain had nothing to do with his or her intentions.

In Western capitalism, the profit motive in itself constitutes what capitalist economic relations are all about. In his praise of the profit motive, Alexis de Tocqueville says, 'The principle of self-interest rightly understood is a lofty one . . . [it] checks one personal interest by another, and uses, to direct the passions, the very same instrument that excites them' (1946, 123). This praise of individual self-seeking is considered vulgar (or *indlamba*) in African thought because it presumes amorality as the main reason for the flourishing of wealth.

The evolution of Western capitalism demanded that human well-being should not be emphasised above the well-being of the economy. To the dismay of Karl Marx, we find the father of population geography, Thomas Malthus, advancing a theory that there is a connection between too many human beings and poverty (1958, 12–15). According to Malthus, an increase in the sum of human mouths gives rise to the depletion of resources. This demographic theory led him to the argument that the poor were not supposed to be helped. A poor person for whom 'at nature's mighty feast there is no cover' (Malthus 1958, 15; Heilbroner 1962, 83) might be kept alive by charity, but since s/he would propagate his/her own kind, such charity can only be cruelty in disguise. Equally, Malthus critiqued what were then called 'Poor Laws' in his English society on the grounds that though these laws may have 'alleviated a little the intensity of individual misfortune, they have spread the evil over a much larger surface' (Malthus 1958, 35). Obviously such a demographic theory shows that the ascendance of Western capitalism went simultaneously with a rejection of the prestige motive.

Karl Marx lamented bitterly the evolution of modern Western capitalism on the grounds that it killed the livelihood and security of the poor that had been entrenched in the prestige motive of traditional society. In the *Communist Manifesto*, which he wrote with Friedrich Engels, he made the following observations:

> The *bourgeoisie*, wherever it has got the upper hand, has put up an end to all feudal, patriarchal, idyllic relations. It has pitilessly torn asunder the motley feudal ties that bound man to his 'natural superiors' and has left no bond between man and man than naked self-interest, than callous cash-payment . . . It has resolved personal worth into exchange value, and in place of the numberless chartered freedom has set up that one unconscionable freedom Free Trade . . . All fixed, fast-frozen relations, with their train of ancient and venerable prejudices, are swept away, all new-formed ones become antiquated before they can ossify. (Marx 1988, 58)

Alfred North Whitehead characterises this evolution of modern Western capitalism as a sociological move from Medievalism to Individualism: 'Feudalism was in full decay, the complex interweaving of church authority with secular government was steadily vanishing. Society could be conceived as functioning in terms of the friendly competition of its individual members, with the State standing as umpire in the minority of instances when there occurred a breakdown of these normal relations' (1948, 114). Furthermore, in the light of this evolution of Western capitalism, 'human progress had been identified with the advance of individualism'. However, Whitehead argues that such a conceptualisation of human progress is flawed because it tends to do away with the reality of the plurality of human values and that individualism could just end in the same way that feudalism ended.

Taking into consideration the fact that Western capitalism works with the presumption that the individual is solely self-interested, it becomes difficult to equate the success of this economic system with ethics. As seen in the preceding discussion, the dominant presumption that dominates all discourse on Western capitalism is that economic relations are only economic when they are driven by the profit motive or personal gain, which is sometimes used interchangeably with self-interest. The prestige motive in post-colonial Africa relativises the profit motive to communal well-being. Jomo Kenyata alludes to this prestige motive in the following passage:

> The selfish or self-regarding man has no name of reputation in the Gikuyu community. An individualist is looked upon with suspicion and is given a nickname of *mwebongia*, one who works for himself and is likely to end up as a wizard. He cannot expect that everything he does will prosper, for the weight of opinion makes him feel his crime against society. Religious sanction works against him, too, for Gikuyu religion is always on the side of solidarity. (1953, 119)

In this way of thinking, the profit motive is incompatible with the prestige motive because the chief moral characteristic of the prestige motive gives precedence to the community before the profit motive. Within the prestige worldview, someone who relates with others solely on the basis of the profit motive is seen as a potential source of evil to the community. But within the traditional African context, the prestige motive was based on the belief that it is through acts of generosity to the community that the individual will flourish. The prestige motive ensures that the community will exist in harmony when wealth is collectively enjoyed (Gelfand 1981, 15; Nyerere 1968, 198–99; Senghor 1964, 29; Kaunda 1966, 29). Traditionally, the profit motive was mainly seen as a source of evil:

> ... in an African context it is very important to share with one's neighbour – whoever does not share withholds the life force from another. Such a person confines oneself to the house and is unable to be a friend to others, thus poisoning the community atmosphere. Neighbours feel bad about such a person and feel that a misfortune is likely to befall him or her. Business enterprises will not flourish, property will be lost, or the family of the owners will be struck by sickness, death or anything. Just in this connection one speaks of sorcery, that is, the neighbour with whom one is unwilling to share may turn into a sorcerer. (Bujo 1998, 162)

According to Bujo, this prestige motive helped to preserve the socio-economic equilibrium within the community because wealth became available to everybody. Thus he writes:

Avarice was one of the most detestable vices. Hence, the border between the avarice and frugality is unclear in Africa, because saving money, for instance, could be taken as an excuse for refusing to offer necessary assistance to others. This may explain why even today people in Africa do not hesitate to organize big feasts with relatives, friends and acquaintances and to spend money lavishly in order to keep human contacts as close as possible. (1998, 163)

Since the prestige motive puts emphasis on communal belonging and acceptability in economic relations, Mazrui argues that 'this prestige motive in traditional societies raises serious economic problems', for example, 'difficulties of trying to get people to save'. In this prestige motive, 'earnings are expended on entertainment and hospitality; on ostentatious weddings, expensive funerals and initiation ceremonies. In addition there is the crippling desire to fulfil obligations towards distant cousins and aunts' (1999, 922).

Mazrui argues further that this prestige motive was partly associated with the post-colonial African state's commitment to socialism or collectivism. A commitment to socialism within a weak economic context in Africa poses a contradiction because, 'if the genius of capitalism is production, the genius of socialism is distribution. And yet one cannot distribute poverty or socialize the means of non-production. Africa will need to develop a productive capacity before it can meaningfully implement a programme of distribution. At least to some extent Africa must become capitalist before it can genuinely become socialist' (Mazrui 1999, 924). Here the argument is that it is a logical impossibility to advocate values of collectivism as required in the prestige motive in a context where people lack that which is supposed to be collectively owned.

Thus some developmental theorists argue that post-colonial Africa needs to adopt an economic attitude that places emphasis on the profit motive, rather than the prestige motive. However, Guy Hunter points out that in African socialism, 'the moral element has been equally strong. It is felt as a revulsion against the sufferings and inequalities of growth as it was achieved in the West; a revulsion particularly against private enterprise, not only because it had been disfigured by greed and exploitation but for its association in Africa – capitalism, imperialism, colonialism'. The African moral element could not be separated from the political and 'purely empirical motives' as demanded by Western capitalism because this moral element was traditional: 'African tribal society and the ethos of the extended family were in many ways egalitarian; certainly the values of personal thrift and competitive personal enterprise were alien to Africa; in this way Africans were worlds apart from the Puritan fathers of America' (1967, 119).

However, Hunter is convinced that the appropriation of Western capitalism in Africa is possible, provided that Africans are willing to realise that 'individual enterprise is not wicked in itself: no one has condemned the will of an individual breadwinner to make a better provision for his own family by his own efforts, and most would agree that this is among the strongest of all human motives. The question is how this can be socialized, so that conscience is not outraged by the inequalities it can produce' (1967, 121–22).

The religious mediation of Western capitalism

Another school of thought suggests that Western capitalism was initially appropriated in African through religious mediation, through the Protestant ethic and Islam. This school of thought derives from Max Weber's thesis that there was an early connection between the Protestant ethics of hard work and frugality and the evolution of modern Western capitalism. Weber's main thesis is that the ascetic form of Protestantism generated the spirit of modern Western capitalism, which is characterised by endless accumulation of wealth, combined with strict discipline. As he puts it: 'In fact, the *summum bonum* of this ethic, the earning of more and more money, combined with the strict avoidance of all spontaneous enjoyment of life . . . Man is dominated by the making of money, by acquisition as the ultimate purpose of life' (1958, 53). Within this religious economic ethic, the rules that came to be seen as indispensable to the working of modern Western capitalism were 'rigid limitation of expenditures on personal consumption or charity, concentration of time and attention to the pursuit of one's business affairs, avoidance of distraction through intimate friendship with others, systematic and pitiless exploitation of labour, and strict observance of honesty in one's relations with others within the limits set by "formal legality"' (48–49; see also Viner 1978, 151; Heilbroner 1962, 54–56). According to Weber, these qualities became indispensable to the evolution of modern Western capitalism as an economic system. Hence the adoption of these strict character qualities in economic relations became part and parcel of the selection of economic subjects 'through a process of economic survival of the fittest' (1958, 55).

Charles van Onselen adopts this Weberian thesis when he says that the appropriation of Western capitalism in Africa was aided by the old churches, rather than the independent African churches, which were considered to be rebellious by the colonial administrators. Religious teachings that emphasised discipline and obedience were welcomed by mine owners as making positive contributions towards the realisation of their mining objectives. Van Onselen writes, 'While remaining basically suspicious, some mining authorities came to realize that not all religious activity was threatening, or incompatible with industrial activity. The majority of religious teachings were conservative, and the values of the protestant ethic, such as obedience and service, could be put to good use in the compounds' (1976, 184–85).

Van Onselen's argument is that religion served to cultivate those virtues that were deemed indispensable for the operation of the mines. Therefore, religion was acceptable and favoured, in so far as it helped in the dissemination of the spirit of Western capitalism. Attributes of a good worker were not restricted to Christianity only. Islam was also acknowledged as a religion that would promote the virtues of Western capitalism:

> Mine managers were also willing to acknowledge that sobriety, hard work and obedience were not exclusively Christian attributes. For the black followers of Islam, who came from Nyasaland, mosques were allowed to be constructed; and at both the Cam & Motor and the Globe and Phoenix mines they became part of compound life. The teachings of Mohammed were considered to meet so well the requirements of industrial life that at the Globe and Phoenix the company undertook to pay the salary of the butcher attached to the mosque . . . (Van Onselen 1976, 186)

In the same vein, Paul Kennedy attributes the absence of entrepreneurial spirit in Africa to the fact that African tradition inhibits the spirit of free enterprise. He writes, 'Thus, entrepreneurs who wish to operate within kinship or community situations, where the social pressures against individual acquisitiveness and mobility are still present and "big men" are expected to redistribute wealth, must find some way to resolve a central contradiction' (1988, 140). Kennedy's argument is that African communalism and its prestige motive was an inhibiting factor in the appropriation of Western capitalism because it did not give room to individual creativity and innovativeness. But Africans who found themselves outside the boundaries of traditional communalism and its prestige motive were able to become successful capitalists. The Christian religion promoted the spirit of entrepreneurship because through conversion to Christianity, these African converts managed to put their business ideas into practice under the guise of religion. According to Kennedy, 'Church membership provided religious justification, spiritual protection and practical assistance for the converts in their struggle to disentangle themselves from the demands of their wider matrikin and concentrate instead on building up their business and nuclear family interests' (1988, 142).

The argument of the religious mediation of Western capitalism hinges on the premise that Africa can only appropriate Western capitalism through emulation of the West. This way of thinking is not new. Sometimes what we see in most of Africa's economic relations is a relentless struggle to keep pace with Western business practices. Mazrui says that African business practices are totally committed 'to emulat[ing] Western methods of production, Western techniques of analysis, Western approaches to organization, and Western styles of behaviour, but in that context of imitation lies the Third World's vulnerability to continuing manipulation of Western economic and political interests' (1982, 252). The idea of emulation is also integral to the dependency theory because it is often argued that African economic well-being depends on Western capitalism and hence an emulation of Western capitalism will lead to Africa's economic independence.

Emulation and the appropriation of Western capitalism
According to Adedeji, most of the theories of development that are used to diagnose Africa's economic development ills are foreign theories derived from Western capitalism. The application of these theories tends to ignore traditional viewpoints of reality and reinforce Africa's economic dependence. Adedeji writes, 'These theories focus attention on such parameters as savings and investments, with insufficient attention to the availability of natural resources, local entrepreneurship, skilled manpower, and technology; and the character dynamics of the domestic market' (1982, 281–82). For Adedeji, a self-sustaining post-colonial African economy should be one that thrives

on making its economic relations more 'place-related' by placing emphasis on values and resources that are offered in the African context. He writes, 'Our development goals and objectives have not been properly guided by our values and perceptions of needs, resources, and possibilities and that there is a dire need for clarification of concepts and definitions, of an understanding of processes and consequences, and of mechanisms for monitoring outcomes and correcting processes and consequences' (1982, 282). Adedeji's argument is that post-colonial African developmental goals have failed to include African values and resources as determinants for its economic relations. The implication of such an argument is that post-colonial African economic relations that are based on the emulation of Western capitalism can only make Africa remain in a vicious circle of dependency.

Hernando de Soto argues that the failure of capitalism in non-Western countries cannot be attributed to culture alone: 'The disparity of wealth between the West and the rest of the world is far too big to be explained by culture alone . . . Many people want the fruits of capital, so much that many . . . are flocking to Western nations' (2000, 4). He goes on to ask: 'If people in countries making a transition to capitalism are not pitiful beggars, are not helplessly trapped in obsolete ways, and are not the uncritical prisoners of dysfunctional cultures, what is it that prevents capitalism from delivering to them the same wealth it has delivered to the West'?

De Soto goes on to claim that non-Western societies do not benefit from capitalism because they have failed to emulate the West in how to produce capital. While non-Western countries 'already possess assets they need to make a success of capitalism, they hold these resources in defective forms: houses built on land whose ownership rights are not adequately recorded, unincorporated businesses with undefined liability, industries located where financiers and investors cannot see them' (2000, 4). According to De Soto, all these economic anomalies imply that while there is ample potential for the creation of wealth in non-Western societies, these anomalies contribute to the failure of the ascendancy of Western capitalism.

But for De Soto, this failure is simply an evolutionary phase in the road to the appropriation of Western capitalism. As he puts it, 'Americans and Europeans have been telling the other countries of the world, "You have to be more like us". In fact they are very much like the United States of a century ago, when it, too, was a Third World country' (2000, 6). The presumption that is being made in De Soto's evolutionary argument is that those people in countries where Western capitalism has not been appropriated are actually existing in a lower state of evolution. Such a lower state of evolution can be discerned from the fact that Western societies were once upon a time living like most of the current underdeveloped non-Western societies (see Hunter 1967, 15).

The idea that all nations should appropriate Western capitalism through emulation hinges also on the assumption that it is the only economic system that humanity has ever known. An evolutionary approach to the appropriation of Western capitalism is also based on the assumption of the ahistorical nature of such an economic system. Western capitalism was not necessarily the result of natural processes of economic evolution. Karl Marx argues that from its embryonic state, modern Western capitalism has always aimed at turning the world to some kind of monolithic existence through its inherent processes of expansiveness. He writes, 'It compels all nations, on pain of extinction, to adopt the bourgeois mode of production; it compels them to introduce what it calls civilization into their midst, i.e., to become bourgeois themselves. In one word, it creates a world after its own image' (1988, 59). The implication of Marx's argument is that the appropriation of Western capitalism is not an inevitable natural process of economic evolution. Rather, it is a process that was deliberately set in motion by modern capitalism as an historical economic system that reduced the diversity of human economic relations to a single system, without taking into consideration the reality of cultural diversities.

The founder of process thought, Alfred North Whitehead echoes the sentiments of Marx from a micro-economic perspective when he says that Western liberal capitalism destroys individuality. As he puts it, 'This destruction is produced by the determined attempt to force completely finished standardized products upon the buyers. The whole motive appealed to is conformation to a standard fashion and not individual satisfaction with the individual thing' (1948, 118).

Anthropological economics and the appropriation of Western capitalism

Anthropological economists argue that economic relations differ from society to society. Hence a proper study of economic relations should focus on societies in their cultural particularity. French anthropologist, Marcel

Mauss, analysed non-Western economic relations from the point of view of society, rather than the individual. In *The Gift*, he advances a thesis that while social solidarity is cemented through the exchange of gifts in pre-capitalist societies, this exchange of gifts operates under the principle of self-interest. He says that what we might perceive as a free gift is just 'polite fiction, formalism, and social deceit' because 'there is obligation and economic self-interest' (1990, 3). The implication of Mauss's anthropological economics is that even those societies that appear to express economic behaviour emphasising mutual concern and solidarity, such economic behaviour is still dominated by self-interest as the main source of motivation. In other words, the tradition of giving in non-Western societies is already a prelude to the market economy that will later evolve into modern Western capitalism.

According to Mausss, what became the dominant characteristic of human economic relations in Western capitalism was something that occurred through the processes of social evolution:

> It is our western societies who have recently made man an 'economic animal'. But we are not yet all creatures of this genus. Among the masses and the elites in our society purely irrational expenditure is commonly practiced. It is still characteristic of a few of the fossilized remnants of our aristocracy. *Homo oeconomicus* is not behind us, but lies ahead, as does the man of morality and duty, the man of science and reason. (1990, 76)

Mauss's anthropological economics seems to imply that the idea of free market economy, populated by individuals who are solely self-interested, as it is entrenched in modern Western capitalism, is the result of a process of evolution. Within this anthropological economic evolutionism, the impression is created that all societies are economically evolving towards the appropriation of Western capitalism.

A different economic anthropological argument that denies the universality of Western capitalism comes from Karl Polanyi. He argues that economic relations of Western capitalism are relative to Western civilisation. He writes: 'The individual in primitive society is not threatened by starvation unless the community as a whole is in like predicament'. To substantiate his argument, he says that among Africans, 'whoever needs assistance receives it unquestioningly' (1968, 163–64). In other words, in African economic relations, a concern for human well-being takes precedence over the profit motive. Since the prestige motive dominates African economic relations, Polanyi argues that Western capitalism was introduced to the Africans through manipulation during the colonial interface, when Africans were exposed to manipulated states of scarcity: 'Thus the colonist may decide to cut the breadfruit trees down in order to create artificial food scarcity or may impose a hut tax on the native to force him to barter away his labour' (1968, 64).

According to Polanyi, it was through this manipulated scarcity that Africans were drawn into Western capitalistic relations that had certain economic behavioural practices that did not exist prior to the colonial interface. To authenticate his argument of cultural relativity of economic behaviour, Polanyi reminds us that 'the motive of individual profit associated with market exchange was never, till the modern age, the dominant principle of economic life' (1968, 56). He further argues that before the advent of modern Western capitalism, traditional societies had economic relations based on 'non-economic relations such as kinship, communal, religious and political relationships' (1968, 56–57). These relations were devoid of the profit motive and material gain.

However, other anthropological economists say that one needs to make a distinction between *homo oeconomicus* entrenched in the theory of Western capitalism and human beings as they really are. The former has been the subject of a heated debate for centuries in the sense that this *homo oeconomicus* did not have a universal existence. Grinker and Steiner are more nuanced on the idea of the cultural relativity of *homo oeconomicus* when they argue that 'Western models of economic behaviour were not applicable to all societies, and more specifically, that the model of the economizing individual, motivated to employ scarce means for the maximum benefit, might not be fruitfully applied to non-capitalist, non-industrial societies' (1997, 89). Within this type of reasoning, we can deduce that while Western capitalism has been successful in Western societies, this does not mean it will equally succeed in all societies. According to Grinker and Steiner, 'certain economic needs are characteristic of particular kinds of societies' (1997, 89). In other words, what might be seen as a formal economic behaviour in one particular society will not necessarily be an economic behaviour in another. If we acknowledge the relativity of economic behaviour, it also implies that instead of emulating Western capitalism, our efforts should rather be focused on domesticating the inherited Western capitalism.

From emulation to the domestication of Western capitalism through humanisation

It is a generally shared school of thought that even after years of intercourse with Western capitalism, it has failed to be appropriated successfully in the African context. The argument that has gone hand in hand with this realisation says that in order for African economic relations to go beyond emulation and dependency, the post-colonially inherited Western capitalism needs to be domesticated or indigenised. According to Mazrui, 'The strategy of indigenization means increasing the utilization of indigenous resources, ranging from native personnel to aspects of traditional local technology' (1982, 253–54). In the process of domesticating the African economy, Mazrui says, 'imported versions of modernity should be more relevant to the local society'. Mazrui's main argument is that emulation kills creativity and innovation because this emulation implies that it will always be the will of the emulated that remains as the immortal truth.

Contemporary discourses on business ethics in post-colonial Africa abound with the idea that African values should be made integral to business practices. All these scholarly endeavours are attempts at domesticating the inherited Western capitalism. There are other scholars who argue that African values should be made integral to the inherited African capitalism. Mike Boon argues that by turning their backs on African traditional values, educated Africans have replaced their traditional values with the worst elements of Western capitalism. Thus he characterises these educated Africans as 'Takers', who are

> ... self-serving and care nothing for the community other than what it can deliver to them personally. They seek to take, not to give or share. Many of these people have managed to educate themselves very well. They know how to manipulate Westerners and how to use, to their own ends, their once-upon-a-time tribe. They are part of the Third World but they also exist in the First World ... Takers have neither integrity nor discipline (1996, 48).

The implication of Boon's argument is that the domestication of Western capitalism in post-colonial Africa is actually retarded by the negative attitude of the 'Takers' towards African traditional values. Whilst African traditional societies would be judged poor through Western eyes, these '[African] tribal societies are socially and morally extremely wealthy, for they have, as part of them, their philosophies in which all people share in the common good' (1996, 48). Boon says that this African traditional outlook towards wealth is sharply contradicted by the African 'Takers' who have developed ferocious appetites for wealth that can only be appeased by endless accumulation. Thus he avers that

> Third World Africa, which is led by Takers, has no discipline. It is not governed according to the same ethics and values as either the First World or the tribal world, and therefore does not respond to them. The Third World Takers are far more insidious and warped than the colonials ever were, yet this is exactly the behaviour and attitude for which colonial settlers were criticized and expelled. The Takers obviously learnt their appalling, self-serving lessons well! (1996, 51)

The implication of Boon's argument is that the economic behaviour of Africa's 'Takers' is detrimental to the appropriation of Western capitalism because such an economic behaviour is a replay of the economic behaviour of the colonialists. According to Boon, an appeal to African traditional values by these 'Takers' is only for self-serving purposes: 'They simply use the tribe to gain their own political ends; they want power, wealth and status, at any cost. The cost is mostly that of the people, the poor humble people who till the lands and work the factories, who dig in the mines and fix the roads' (1996, 52). In other words, by refusing to include African values in their business dealings, 'Takers' cause suffering among ordinary Africans.

For many African scholars and politicians who are staunch believers in African humanistic values, the element of individual acquisitiveness and the compromising of communal well-being inherent in Western capitalism raises moral questions. Julius Nyerere says: 'The creation of wealth is a good thing and something which we shall have to increase. But it will cease to be good the moment when wealth ceases to serve human beings and begins to be served by human beings' (1968, 319). Nyerere's rebuke of Western capitalism is primarily based on the humanist communitarian ethic that exists in African traditional society, where community needs take precedence over individual self-gratification. Within this ethic, he argues that the means for acquiring wealth should enhance human dignity, instead of dehumanising people. Thus an appeal to *ujamaa* (a Swahili term, which means 'familyhood') as the guiding national development policy was partly intended to do away with dependence on the bounties of Western capitalism that has always manifested itself in the form of aid.

To avoid such dependence, Nyerere argues that Africa's economic relations should be domesticated. As he puts it, 'we have to think in terms of what is available, or can be made available, at comparatively small cost, and which can be operated by people. By moving into the future along this path, we can avoid massive social disruption and human suffering' (1968, 320). Where Western capitalism claimed that economic relations had nothing to do with humanistic sentiments of fellow feeling, Nyerere insists on the importance of incorporating such African values into economic relations. Here it should be noted that focus is given to human well-being for the sake of it.

While Western capitalism would recommend that the economy would do well by even sacrificing the well-being of the majority of the citizenry, Nyerere argues that African humanistic values give primacy to the well-being of all the citizens to such an extent that even technology applied in the process of production is only justifiable when it embraces wider social participation. He writes, 'We have to consider whether some older equipment which demands more labour, but labour which is less highly skilled, is not better suited to our needs, as well as being more within our capacity to build and use' (1968, 312). Obviously this type of thinking is completely the opposite of Western capitalism, with its tendency to emphasise productivity through maximum efficiency. Western capitalism says that for a firm to be efficient and productive, it should apply the best technological equipment available and do away with costs that threaten the maximisation of its profits. Retrenchments of workers by companies is a common example of this rationale.

The economic ideals of *ujamaa* are echoed by Jomo Kenyata in his socio-economic policy of *harambee*. In Swahili, *harambee* means 'to pull together, or to work together or to pull the same rope together, at the same time' (cited in Bujo 1998, 164). Kenyata interpreted the political independence of Kenya as implying the dawn of an era of *harambee*. The presumption behind *harambee*'s economic policy was that when people pool all their talents for a common cause, such as poverty alleviation, they are able to promote the well-being of everybody, more than when each one is concerned with his/her own gain. Kenyata says that in African society 'there is no really individual affair, for everything has a moral and social reference. The habit of corporate effort is but the other side of corporate ownership; and corporate responsibility is illustrated in corporate work no less than in corporate sacrifice' (1953, 119).

Obviously an economic system such as Western capitalism that does not begin with a commitment to solidaristic communalism will be unintelligible when subjected to a cultural context that emphasises communal solidarity, rather than individual independence or autonomy from community (Gyekye 1997, 52). Kwasi Wiredu confirms this incompatibility, saying, 'One of the greatest problems facing us in Africa is how to reap the benefits of industrialization without incurring the more unlovable of its apparent fallouts, such as the ethic of austere individualism' (1996, 71). But Kwame Gyekye does not agree with the emphasis that has been put on African communalism. Among his criticisms of those who espoused African communalism are the arguments that African traditional society allowed individual dexterity and private property, and secondly that African traditional religion itself is materialistic:

> The acquisitive, capitalistic elements of the African character, the hankering after material welfare, the appreciation of wealth and material success: all these attitudes have reverberations in the African conception and practice of religion. In African traditional conceptions, religion is to be pursued also for its social or material relevance. Supernatural beings are to be worshiped because of the succour they could, and are expected to, provide for the human being in his this-worldly, mundane pursuits; the munificence of the gods was to be exploited for human well-being in this world. (1997, 155)

The implication of Gyekye's argument is that African traditional religion is imbued with many of the same elements as Western capitalism because of its materialistic outlook. In other words, the religiosity of Africans is inseparable from their perpetual yearning for material success. According to Gyekye, African religion and culture are not incompatible with Western capitalism, especially when it comes to the idea of accumulation and the institution of private property. He attributes the failure of Western capitalism to colonialism because 'colonial governments seem to have adopted policies and measures that palpably ran counter to the ideas and values of individual enterprise and the free market system' (1997, 157).

On the future of capitalism in post-colonial Africa

In order to go beyond emulation, it is imperative that post-colonial Africa comes to terms with the fact that its own cultural values are incompatible with capitalist modes of thinking and the Western conceptualisation of a human being. As we have seen in the above discussion, the idea of a solely self-interested individual as the ideal businessperson is incompatible with the traditional African moral conviction that a person is communal by nature and that he/she depends on the well-being of others, in as much as others depend on his or her well-being. Within this trend of thought, it also follows that economic relations must be sensitised to the well-being of the whole community, instead being solely premised on individual acquisitiveness and self-aggrandisement.

We have also seen that practical efforts towards the domestication of Western capitalism in post-colonial Africa were expressed in some of the post-colonial African social economic policies, such as *ujamaa*, *harambee* and sometimes in what was called African socialism. Since the demise of socialism elsewhere in the world, these post-colonial African economic policies have been replaced with policies such as indigenisation, Africanisation and black economic empowerment (BEE). The pursuit of these socio-economic policies shows an effort to domesticate and contextualise inherited Western capitalism in post-colonial Africa. The aim of these policies is basically that Africans must own and control capitalism within their own social, cultural and political context. Here the conviction is that Africans should determine capitalism, rather than having to deal with an economic system that is externally determined.

From a theoretical perspective, the need to domesticate capitalism has also given rise to the inclusion of African humanistic discourses in post-colonial business practices. Post-colonial African scholars, especially post-apartheid South African scholars, have maintained that African values such as those enshrined in the ethic of *ubuntu* should be made integral to business practices in post-apartheid South Africa. The main presumption is that it is through the inclusion of African humanistic values such as being concerned with the needs of others, being sensitive to religious and cultural beliefs of others and a total commitment to the well-being of all would enable humane economic relations.

Select bibliography

Adedeji, A. 1982. 'Development and Economic Growth in Africa to the Year 2000: Alternative Projections and Policies'. In *Alternative Futures for Africa*, ed. T. Shaw, 279–304. Colorado: Westview Press.

Boon, M. 1996. *The African Way: The Power of Interactive Leadership*. Johannesburg: Zebra Press.

Bujo, B. 1998. *The Ethical Dimension of Community: The African Model and the Dialogue Between North and South*. Limuru: Kolbe Press.

Davis, R.H. 1973. 'Interpreting the Colonial Period in African History'. *African Affairs* 72 (289): 383–400.

De Soto, H. 2000. *The Mystery of Capital: Why Capitalism Triumphs in the West and Fails Everywhere Else*. London: Bantam.

De Tocqueville, A. 1946. *Democracy in America: Vol. II*. Eds. F. Bowen and P. Bradley. New York: Alfred Knopf.

Gelfand, M. 1981. *Ukama: Reflections on Shona and Western Cultures in Zimbabwe*. Gweru: Mambo Press.

Goldsmith, M.M. 1985. *Private Vices, Public Benefits: Bernard Mandeville's Social and Political Thought*. Cambridge: Cambridge University Press.

Grinker, R.R. and C.B. Steiner (eds.). 1997. *Perspectives on Africa: A Reader in Culture, History and Representation*. London: Blackwell.

Gross, F. 1956. *Rhodes of Africa*. London: Cassell.

Gyekye, K. 1997. *Tradition and Modernity: Philosophical Reflections on African Experience*. New York: Oxford University Press.

Heilbroner, R.L. 1962. *The Making of Economic Society*. Englewood Cliffs: Prentice Hall.

Hunter, G. 1967. *The Best of Both Worlds? A Challenge on Development Policies in Africa*. London: Oxford University Press.

Iliffe, J. 1983. *The Emergence of African Capitalism*. London: Macmillan.

Johnston, H.H. 1913. *A History of the Colonisation of Africa by Alien Races*. Cambridge: Cambridge University Press.

Kaunda, K. 1966. *A Humanist in Africa*. London: The Camelot Press.

Keigwin, H.S. 1923. 'Native Development'. *The Southern Rhodesia Native Affairs Department Annual* 1 (2/6) (December): 10–17.

Kennedy, P. 1988. *African Capitalism: The Struggle for Ascendancy.* Cambridge: Cambridge University Press.
Kenyata, J. 1953. *Facing Mount Kenya.* London: Secker and Warburg.
Leys, C. 1994. 'African Capitalists and Development: Theoretical Questions'. In *African Capitalists in African Development*, eds. B.J. Berman and C. Leys, 11–38. London: Lynne Rienner Publishers.
Lux, K. 1990. *Adam Smith's Mistake: How a Moral Philosopher Invented Economics and Ended Morality.* London: Shambhala.
Magee, S.P. 2000. 'Bioeconomics: Lessons for Business, Nations and Life'. In *The Complexity Vision and the Teaching of Economics*, ed. D. Colander, 255–84. Cheltenham: Edward Edgar Publishing.
Malthus, T.R. 1958 [1826]. *An Essay on the Principle of Population as it Affects the Future Improvement of Society.* London: John Murray.
Mandeville, B. 1924. *The Fable of the Bees, Vol. 2.* Ed. F.B. Kaye. Oxford: Oxford University Press.
Marquard, L. and T.G. Standing. 1939. *The Southern Bantu.* London: Oxford University Press.
Marx, K. 1988. *The Communist Manifesto.* Ed. F.L. Bender. New York: Rider.
Mauss, M. 1990. *The Gift: The Form and Reason for Exchange in Archaic Societies.* Trans. W.E. Halls. New York: W.W. Norton.
Mazrui, A.A. 1966. *On Heroes and Uhuru-Worship: Essays on Independent Africa.* London: Green.
———. 1980. *The African Condition: A Political Diagnosis.* London: Heinemann.
———. 1982. 'The Computer Culture and Nuclear Power: Political Implications for Africa'. In *Alternative Futures for Africa*, ed. T.T. Shaw, 237–58. Colorado: Westview Press.
———. 1990. 'Nation-Building and Changing Political Values'. In *General History of Africa VIII: Africa Since 1935*, eds. A.A. Mazrui and C. Wondji, 435–98. London: James Currey.
———. 1999. 'Towards the Year 2000'. In *General History of Africa VIII: Africa Since 1935*, eds. A.A. Mazrui and C. Wondji, 905–34. London: James Currey.
Mihevc, J. 1995. *The Market Tells Them So: The World Bank and Economic Fundamentalism in Africa.* London: Zed.
Mosley, P. (ed.). 1991. *Aid and Power: The World Bank and Policy-Based Lending, Vol. I.* London: Routledge.
Mudenge, S.I.G. 1988. *A Political History of Munhumutapa c.1400–1902.* London: James Currey.
Murove, M.F. 1999. 'The Shona Concept of *Ukama* and the Process Philosophical Concept of Relatedness, with Special Reference to the Ethical Implications of Contemporary Neo-Liberal Economic Practices'. Masters thesis, University of Natal, Pietermaritzburg.
Nyerere, J.K. 1968. *Freedom and Socialism: Uhuru na Ujamaa.* Oxford: Oxford University Press.
Polanyi, K. 1968. *The Great Transformation: The Political and Economic Origins of Our Time.* New York: Renehart.
Radcliffe, T. 1994. 'Jurassic Park or Last Supper'. *The Tablet*, 18 June: 761–63.
Samkange, S. and T.M. Samkange. 1980. *Hunhuism or Ubuntuism: A Zimbabwean Indigenous Political Philosophy.* Harare: The Graham Publishing Company.
Sender, J. and S. Smith. 1986. *The Development of Capitalism in Africa.* London: Methuen.
Senghor, L.S. 1964. *On African Socialism.* London: Macmillan.

Smith, A. 1976. *An Inquiry into the Nature and Causes of the Wealth of Nations.* Eds. R.H. Campbell, A.S. Skinner and W.B. Todd. New York: Modern Library.
Theron, S. 1995. *Africa, Philosophy and the Western Tradition: An Essay in Self-Understanding.* Frankfurt: Peter Lang GmbH.
Vambe, L. 1972. *An Ill-Fated People: Zimbabwe Before and After Rhodes.* London: Heinemann.
Van Onselen, C. 1976. *Chibaro: African Mine Labour in Southern Rhodesia 1900–1933.* London: Pluto Press.
Veblen, T. 1931. *The Theory of the Leisure Class: An Economic Study of Institutions.* New York: The Modern Library.
Viner, J. 1978. *Religious Thought and Economic Society.* Eds. J. Melitz and D. Winch. Durham: Duke University Press.
Weber, M. 1958. *The Protestant Ethic and the Spirit of Capitalism.* London: Allen and Unwin.
Whitehead, A.N. 1948. *Essays in Science and Philosophy.* New York: Rider and Co.
Wilson, N.H. 1923. 'The Development of Native Reserves: One Phase of Native Policy for Southern Rhodesia'. *Native Affairs Department Annual* 1 (2/6) (December): 86–94.
Wiredu, K. 1996. *Cultural Universals and Particulars: An African Perspective.* Bloomington: Indiana University Press.

6

Ethics, African Societal Values and the Workplace

JOHN MTYUWAFHETHU MAFUNISA

THE DEVELOPMENT OF a work ethic indigenous to African people is essential for effective and efficient work performance by employees in Africa. Employees' attitudes towards their work have been shaped through a period of time. They can be traced back to their early childhood experiences, which are then passed on to the next generation through various value systems, including ethics, mores, traditions, customs and conversions. It is the duty of all members of the society to instil a work ethic and attitudes in children, so that they will not depart from them when they are adults and members of the economic workforce. Our question is: Are there particular African ethics or societal values that influence an indigenous African work ethic?

The label 'African' is potentially problematic if defined in purely geographical terms, referring to all the inhabitants of the continent of Africa, irrespective of race and colour. However, when the definition rests on the classificatory framework based exclusively on race and colour, it could be viewed as another form of apartheid (Maylam 1986, iv). In terms of their social identity, Africans are diverse people, related through history, culture and the consciousness of being Africans in the world (Armah 1999, xi). The geographical identity that is often used, excludes other Africans making a living outside the African continent, although historically, culturally and otherwise, their African identity is not questionable. The geographical definition imposes formidable challenges in this period of time, where the question of identity is crucial. In this chapter, the label 'African' is not limited to race, colour and geographical location, but extends to attributes such as consciousness, shared values and history. Thus we use a broad definition, inclusive of all Africans in an enquiry of this nature where values constitute a point of reference. In addition, the contextualisation of the guidelines of social values is within African communities and not the African continent. There are Western communities, for example, on the African continent, that do not subscribe to the African values, just as there are African communities in other parts of the world that do not subscribe to Western, Indian, Chinese values, etc.

African societal values can be defined as values that are congruent with the values of the indigenous population. Legum contends that when authors write about Africa, consideration should be given as to whether they are referring to Africa as perceived through African or Western eyes of the mind (1999, 2). In this chapter, the selected primary values are discussed fundamentally as perceived through African eyes. Selected primary African societal values will be identified and discussed, namely: communalisation, *ubuntu*, traditionalism, oral tradition and religion. An attempt will be made to link these African societal values to the behaviour of Africans in the workplace, and particularly to Africans working in the public service. This then is the subject of this chapter: How can public officials who work with Africans, for example in community upliftment projects, persuade and encourage Africans to work with them and to work hard?

Defining ethics, values and African societal values
Ethics are rules or standards governing the moral conduct of members of a society – whether they are employees in an institution, or members of an association, or a group, or any other societal cluster. Ethics deals with values relating to human conduct, with respect to the rightness or wrongness of particular actions and the motives and ends of such actions. Rightness refers to what ought to be, or what is approved of and wrongness refers to what ought not to be, or what is disapproved of by the society (Mafunisa 2000a, 79). It can be argued that ethics is concerned not only with distinguishing right from wrong and good from bad, but also with the commitment to do what is right or acceptable to the society or institution concerned. A value can be seen as something highly regarded by someone. What one person regards or esteems highly may differ from what another person regards as important (Mafunisa 2000b, 247). Thus, public work affecting communities needs to take cognisance of what the community approves or disapproves of.

All societies develop ethics based on societal custom and such group morality helps to preserve shared values. Almost universal among societies are customary negative values – neglect and cruelty toward children, treachery toward family and the community and murder (especially of one's family or other members of the community). Other behaviour almost universally seen in a positive light includes parental care and respect for other people. Conformity to societal values is not enforced by law, but by a socially binding force. These values are followed because their practical utility is recognised by reason and testified to by the experience of members of the community. Also, injunctions of how to behave when associating with friends, relatives, superiors, equals at work and so on, are obeyed, because any deviation from them makes a human being feel and look in the eyes of others, ridiculous and socially uncouth (Manning and Curtis 1988, 67–68). Let us now turn to a discussion of selected primary values in African society.

Communalisation of human life
According to Rasheed and Olowu, African societies value the communalisation of human life, rather than the privatisation that Western society values (1993, 17). In the Western tradition, human life is seen in terms of separation, independence and conflict. Separateness is treasured and regarded as intrinsic to the integrity of human life. Only when it is privatised, does human life have identity, autonomy and freedom. In contrast, African traditions regard human life as communal. People have identity because they belong to a community. Their freedom lies in the capabilities, privileges and immunities that derive from communal life. Honesty lies in the location of an individual in a community and the ways in which the individual manages the entitlements and obligations of community membership. These statements are echoed by Setiloane, who states that in the myth about the genesis of earthly life, Africans invariably teach that the first appearance of people was as a group (1988, 9). They came about in a community of men, women and children. The extended family is a proverbial African expression and an African village community is like a large family: every person is related to another. These relationships by marriage, blood, or by mere associations are emotionally based and are traditionally cherished. This becomes evident when a need arises, as in the case of death, or some occasion for rejoicing, such as a wedding. Funerals and clan festivals bring the communal people together in one place (of

worship). The worship of these occasions is invariably enactment of traditional ritual.

In traditional African communities, life revolves around a collective body. A collective body can be a tribe, a village and in most cases, the extended family. In these settings, formal and informal rules and customs are developed to advance the primacy of the collective. The extended family is the base upon which a village is formed. From the village, various tribes of ethnic groupings develop up to the level of the community and maximise the development to the level of a society. Tshikwatamba argues that this development is referred to as the collective chain of humanity (2003, 10). From colonialism to constitutional dispensations, African states bonded within the bounds of collectivism and consolidated their efforts in political struggle through slogans such as 'an injury to one is an injury to all'.

These sentiments emanate from collectivism, a cultural value of African people, although it was never accepted or implemented under colonialism. Around the globe, Africans perceive themselves as part of a collective and accept that their collective destiny as Africans is at stake. Of course, there are limits to collectivism – for example, Tshikwatamba does not side with those African students in higher education institutions who seemed to be manipulating this collectivism when they assumed the slogan of 'pass one, pass all' (2004, 262).

Tshikwatamba promotes the idea of collective management and defines it as an African value-laden practice of decision-making by the collective body for the benefit of all within the spirit of *ubuntu* (2003, 3). He draws a distinction between participative management and collective management. The latter is more African, while the former is more Western. While participative and collective management styles are towards the same end of a continuum, and while participative management requires input from many people in the organisation, collective management goes further and strives to involve the whole organisation in making a final decision. The African Renaissance requires that this value be repositioned in the mainstream.

Lapin shows how studies confirm that when the traditions of workers are ignored and alienated, it impacts adversely on efficiency and productivity (1992, 19). In the apartheid past, institutional culture in South Africa was autocratically dictated by the value systems and cultures of non-Africans, who ran the country's public and private institutions and effectively enforced their usage and insisted on adherence to them. These cultures assumed specific values and ethics and it was further assumed that everyone would comply with these values and ethics. The fact is, however, that one cannot compel ethical compliance if the ethics are not congruent with the value system and culture of the individual concerned and at no point was apartheid successful in transmitting a work ethic to which the total workforce became committed.

Lapin argues further that what we need to do now is to develop a work ethic that is congruent with and indigenous to the various value systems and traditions operating in South African workplaces. While there are indeed diverse cultures in South Africa, each with its own value system, these divergent value systems do share some common universal values – for example, that stealing is wrong. Thus if a work ethic could be constructed out of those universal values, rather than from the values of specific cultures, South Africa would have an ethic to which the entire workforce would be committed. This requires, however, that African values be taken into serious consideration, along with the values of other cultures.

Rasheed and Olowu argue that the communalisation of life is an alternative and legitimate way of looking at life and is a major asset to be used in developing a national common ethos (1993, 18). An example of African communalisation would be *stokvels*, a sort of informal savings club common in African societies, where individuals pool their savings in order to gain better returns, and sometimes make loans to individual members of the group from the pooled savings. Communalisation encourages collective consumption of wealth, as opposed to individual consumerism. It has a strong element of social solidarity against corruption by political office-bearers and employees. Most importantly, it is the basis of the community self-help projects that have been the driving force in the development of rural Africa. It is through these self-help projects that Africans have acquired skills such as human or interpersonal relations, conflict resolution and motivating others to achieve high levels of performance.

Ubuntu

Closely related to the notion of the communalisation of life is the concept of *ubuntu*. A belief in *ubuntu* can enable Africans to respect the values of all members of South African society and to realise that a person exists to serve others. Mbigi and Maree suggest that *ubuntu* is a metaphor that describes the significance of group solidarity that is so central to the survival of African communities, who as a result of poverty and deprivation have to survive through brotherly care from a group and not individual self-reliance (1995, 1). In essence, *ubuntu* is a universal concept that can be applicable to all African people. An example of group solidarity in the Limpopo Province is that of clearing, weeding and harvesting in Vhavenda that is often done in a semi-communal way. A large quantity of traditional beer is prepared and all members of the community are invited to join in the work and afterwards in the drinking of beer. This is a popular and efficient way of lightening arduous work and appears to be a fundamental part of the Vhavenda agricultural system (Stayt 1968, 35).

Traditional African communities thrive on the principles of *ubuntu* – essentially a divine inspiration that enables African people to act according to socio-cultural norms and values based on the existence of their inner being. This inner being is understood to be the centre of human personalities, feelings, thoughts and will. It can be argued that *ubuntu* is the inner inspiration that comes from the heart, the inner being and the centre of human values. *Ubuntu* can be understood as the essence of God's presence within humanity and the manifestation of God to humanity (Mulemfo 2000, 57). There is no equivalent term in Western languages that translates the meaning of *ubuntu* in the true African sense. It is, however, a value common to all African ethnic groupings. Although *ubuntu* is referred to here in isiZulu, Sotho-speaking people refer to it as *botho*, while the Vhavenda people refer to it as *vhuthu*. Mbigi states that in Shona, the concept of *ubuntu* is known as *unhu* (1995, 3).

It is useful to refer to expressions such as, 'A man is only a man through the other; I am because we are'. Thus, one has to encounter the 'we', before discovering the 'I' (Mbigi 1995, 10). The 'I' does not exist in isolation from the collective. A clear example of this is the *ubuntu*-loaded sentiments of former Zambian president, Kenneth Kaunda, during the birth of the Zambian nation in 1964, when he addressed the nation and said that if the attainment of independence was to have meaningful consequences, the individual human being should always be a priority to ensure that he or she does not become a meaningless cog in the wheel, but a keystone on which development hinges. Kaunda argued that Zambia's independence had been achieved to plan for a better future for the people and that the word 'people' is rather abstract unless converted to the single unit. Thus, at its root, the word 'people' refers to man (or woman). Sometimes material development has been so emphasised by non-Africans that plans to advance more and more in a material way have become more important than the welfare of individual men or women for whom these plans for the future are made (Van Rensburg cited in Tshikwatamba 2004, 261). Another example is the traditional African belief relating to old people. There is no traditional belief in relegating senior citizens to old age homes, as is common in Western communities. Traditionally, the older the senior citizens become, the more they should be respected, taken care of and dignified within the family unit and the entire collective. In the primary cultures of the African people, the social status of a person is not a fundamental consideration, but the focus is rather on his or her humanity within which *ubuntu* is to be found.

In rendering services to African communities, public employees should ensure that the fundamental proverbial principles of *ubuntu* are not violated. Public functionaries should carry out their duties with great care and pay attention to details, so as to foster a spirit of unconditional acceptance and care of the entire person, regardless of the social status of a particular individual or community.

Traditionalism
Traditionalism deals with adherence to the doctrines or practices of traditions, or the beliefs of those opposed to modernism or liberalism. It is an African normative value that maintains customs, mores and living patterns that have been established over time. Keulder states that traditionalism commonly refers to that which is old (2000, 151). According to Max Weber, tradition is the authority of the 'eternal yesterday', i.e. of the mores sanctified through the unimaginably ancient recognition and habitual orientation to conform (Tshikwatamba 2004, 263). Traditionalism is a set of rituals or symbolic practices normally governed by overtly or tacitly accepted rules to inculcate particular values and norms of behaviour by repetition. New traditions are likely to be invented when rapid transformation of a society weakens or destroys the social patterns for which old traditions have been designed, or when such old traditions and their institutional carriers and promulgators no longer prove sufficiently adaptable and flexible. Thus traditionalism emphasises a lifestyle and value system that evolves and progresses over time. It implies the continuity of ideas, values and institutions transmitted from generation to generation.

The Constitution of the Republic of South Africa (Act 108 of 1996) acknowledges traditional leadership, thereby stipulating that the institution, status and role of traditional leaders operating according to customary law are recognised, subject to the Constitution of the country. Traditional leaders are the custodians of the traditionalism, cultures, customs and values. Leaders enjoy the legitimacy of particular communities to direct their affairs, but their legitimacy is based on tradition that includes the whole range of inherited culture and way of life. People's history, moral and social values and traditional institutions survive to serve those values.

Jacob Zuma argues that the government regards traditional leaders as custodians of the moral, value, cultural and social systems of many people in South Africa. Traditional institutions embody the preservation of the culture, traditions, customs and values of African people and represent early forms of social institutions and governance (Zuma 2008).

African orientation towards the past suggests that present events should relate to the historical past. The past represents the final destiny (Oosthuizen 1985, 98). Its importance is crucial in understanding the present and the future. It is acceptable within African communities that people's views about the present state of affairs should inevitably contain built-in assumptions about the past. Their present preoccupations and considerations are determined to a great extent by the way in which the past is related. In the case of present-day South Africa, the advantages of connecting with the past reveal a sharp contrast between a white dominated-developed capitalist economic sector and an impoverished African rural sector (Maylam 1986, viii).

From the premise that public institutions should promote the welfare of the community (Tshikwatamba 2004, 264), public employees should therefore always be fair and reasonable in their interactions with each citizen, regardless of race, language or belief system. In this context, the guidelines of 'fairness and reasonableness' must include the full recognition of traditionalism and consideration of the living patterns of Africans and their desire to connect with the past. Public employees must not to be judgemental concerning the manifestation of traditionalism while they interact with African communities. A typical example where traditionalism was recognised to promote the guidelines of 'fairness' and 'reasonableness' as a means of relating to the past is with the establishment of the Truth and Reconciliation Commission in South Africa. It was considered fair and reasonable to establish the Commission to heal the ill feelings of the past, affording an opportunity to the victims of apartheid to reconcile themselves with past experiences.

Oral tradition

Oral tradition is an important cultural value and can be regarded as the oldest form of narrating history. It manifests itself in the historical consciousness of pre-literate societies and has a functional character. It is the most effective way to narrate social and community history and addresses the needs of the most disadvantaged and illiterate. Oral tradition became the taproot in the new interdisciplinary method designed to serve the purpose of researching the continent's past. The fact that it became a method suitable to Africa does not mean that it is limited to the African continent. Thus most of the information coded in written references is also captured from oral sources.

African communities, particularly those with hereditary dynasties, engage individual members in memorisation, recitation and the passing on of oral history from one generation to the other. In some African communities, recitations are often accompanied with the music of stringed instruments, while in other communities, oral tradition is regarded as a fixed text. Revered customs and traditions find validity in the present by being associated with an oral tradition.

According to Thompson, oral tradition can change the focus of history and open new areas of research (1978, 2). It can be divided into various categories. The formulae category comprises proverbs, slogans, phrases, riddles and epigrams. The second category is poems and songs. Poetry fulfils an aesthetic demand with regard to form and content, while formulae are merely instrumental in the performance of an act of some kind. The third category is a list of places, people and dates recited at public meetings, such as funerals and religious festivals. The fourth category consists of tales that exist in prose form and serve as the source of relating series of events (Vansina 1965, 150–52).

Africans often express their societal values through proverbs, where the oldest forms of African societal values can be found (Mbiti 1989, 29). For example, Vhavenda warns its tribal members: '*Munwe muthihi a u tusi mathuthu*' (One finger cannot pick stamped mealies), which translates as, 'A person can't perform many jobs alone'. It means that in Vhavenda social custom, people's values and needs can only be promoted effectively by a unified effort by all members of the society. In Vhavenda social custom, also, the instilling of ethical work values is not only the responsibility of parents, but of all members of the society. This is best expressed by the following proverb: *'Tsiwana i laiwa ndilani'* (An orphan is given advice on the way). It means that every member of the society is given advice on personal, familial, religious and work values by all members of the society (Mafunisa 2000a, 258).

Written records may prove to be inefficient on their own. Oral tradition is derived primarily from those who cannot read and write, and hence the majority of the African scholars take pride in this tradition. Although able to read and write, African scholars may still prefer the oral method to the written method to pass on information to and from one another. Should they pass on information in written form, they may still make an oral follow-up to confirm the written information (Tshikwatamba 2004, 266). Efficiency and effectiveness are some of the basic values and principles of public administration emanating from societal values. It may be more effective to make use of oral communication when passing on information from one employee to another, particularly with employees who are unable to read and write. For these employees, oral communication may not be a question of choice, but of necessity.

Religion
Africans are religious, and even each tribe has its own religious system with a set of beliefs and practices. Reference is made to African traditional religions in the plural because there are, Mbiti argues, about three thousand tribes, and each has its own religious system (1989, 1). To ignore these beliefs, attitudes and practices can only lead to a lack of understanding of African behaviour and problems in the workplace. The Research Institute for Theology and Religion argues that African traditional religion is a way of life and a search for well-being within the community in the here and now of everyday existence. It encompasses beliefs concerning a supreme being, ancestors and the mediation of diviners and/or rainmakers.

To black Africans, it is the ancestors, elders and priests who are the daily guardians or police of human morality. Social regulations of a moral nature are directed towards the immediate contact between individuals, and between human beings and ancestral spirits. The list of social regulations includes the following: do not kill another human being (except in a war); do not steal; do not show disrespect to people of higher status; do not backbite; do not tell lies and do not despise or laugh at cripples. In positive language, the list includes terms such as: be kind; help those who cry to you for help; show *ubuntu*; be faithful in marriage; respect elders; keep justice; behave in a humble way towards those senior to you and follow the customs and traditions of your community (Mbiti 1989, 208–09).

The belief in continued life after death forms the basis of the real and vital religion of some of the Pedi and Vhavenda peoples. The direct relationship with dead ancestors, or 'gods' (*badimo* or *midzimu*) is a personal factor in their lives and is the basis of their religious ideas. Veneration of the ancestors is conducted mainly through prayer and sacrifice. Usually these two elements are combined in the same ritual, which is called '*phasa badimo*', or in Tshivenda, '*u phasela midzimu*' (to sacrifice to the ancestors). *Badimo* or *midzimu* can communicate back to Pedis or Vhavenda through dreams. This is the regular method of intercession for some Pedis and Vhavenda for blessings at work and everywhere they are. The blessings include promotion and salary increment (Mafunisa 1998, 131).

To the Pedi and Vhavenda people, who are adherents of African traditional religions, a lack of respect towards one's superior at home, in the community, or at work implies a lack of respect for ancestors. If one does not respect people during one's lifetime, one will also not respect them after their death. Similarly, a person who does not respect his/her parents is not fit to join them after his/her death. Of all the forms of respect expected of a person, the respect due to the ancestors is regarded as the greatest of them all. The ancestral spirits cause the supernatural sanctions that are brought into operation by an act of sin. The normal precautionary measure or remedy is sacrifice.

According to Tshikwatamba, matters of spiritualism are closely related to religion. The Constitution of South Africa shifted from Christian values to religious values that accommodate all religious practices that were suppressed in the past, particularly the religious practices of the indigenous African people that were hindered by the long domination of colonialism. Colonial missionaries introduced Christianity and Islam in Africa and unsuccessfully attempted to destroy African spiritualism. Their attempts were unsuccessful because Africans accepted Christianity and Islam, not as a replacement of African religion, but as a new perspective to be added to a stock of historically accumulated perspectives. African Christians, for example, did not allow African religion to be Christianised; rather they Africanised and indigenised Christianity (2004, 267).

Western civilisation declared traditional practices barbaric, although they are important for the majority of the workforce in the public sector. The resuscitation of these practices requires central positioning in the African Renaissance programme to address the holistic question of self-identity and acknowledgement. Tshikwatamba has deduced that African spiritualism is a primary value among Africans, while other Western values imposed on Africans by missionaries are of a secondary status (2004, 267). This discussion moves from the premise that contextualisation of guidelines for public administration within African communities requires being cognisant of African spiritualism and that such a value should not be treated with contempt. For example, when projects are to be implemented in specific geographical areas, religious considerations may sometimes require community members to consult with ancestors regarding the feasibility of the projects. This is carried out to ensure that a harmonious relationship is sustained between the spirit world and the world of the ancestors and the community.

Conclusion
The solution to Africa's current negative work ethic lies in learning from those public employees who successfully find a happy medium between African societal values and their employers' demands for productivity. When training future African public employees, one can no longer ignore the fact that their mentality is often affected more by the ideal of the common good, than by the importance of individual performance, which has been imported from North American management models. African senior employees need to try to integrate Western managerial logic and African social ideals, rather than seeing them as incompatible opposites. A study on preparing African leaders shows that it would be more profitable for African managerial trainees to be educated about inevitable culture clash between different management models (Mutabazi 2002).

As argued in this chapter, the need exists to develop a work ethic congruent with and indigenous to the various value systems and traditions operating in South African workplaces. Thus, if a work ethic could be constructed out of universal values, rather than from the values of a few cultures, South Africa would be able to develop a work ethic to which the entire workforce would be committed.

Select bibliography

Armah, A.K. (ed.). 1999. *The New Struggle in African Renaissance*. Cape Town: Mafube.
Gerth, H. and C. Mill. 1946. *From Max Weber: Essays in Sociology*. New York: Cambridge University Press.
Keulder, C. 2000. *Traditional Leaders in State-Society and Democracy: A Reader in Namibian Politics*. Windhoek: Macmillan.
Lapin, D. 1992. 'A Sense of Values'. *Finance Week* 55 (10): 19–21.
Legum, C. 1999. *Africa Since Independence*. Bloomington: Indiana University Press.
Mafunisa, M.J. 1998. 'The Development of Positive Work Ethic in the Public Service with Specific Reference to the Northern Province'. Ph.D. dissertation, faculty of Economic and Management Sciences, University of Pretoria.
———. 2000a. *Public Service Ethics*. Kenwyn: Juta.
———. 2000b. 'Positive Work Ethic: A Multicultural Perspective'. *Journal of Public Administration* 35 (4): 245–60.
Manning, G. and K. Curtis. 1988. *Ethics at Work*. New York: South-Western Publishing Co.
Maylam, P. 1986. *A History of the African People of South Africa: From the Early Iron Age to the 1970s*. Cape Town: Creda Press.
Mbigi, I. 1995. '*Ubuntu* in the Workplace'. *Productivity SA* (July/August): 10–12.
Mbigi, I. and J. Maree. 1995. *Ubuntu: The Spirit of Transformation Management*. Pretoria: Knowledge Resources.
Mbiti, J. 1989. *African Religions and Philosophy*. Pretoria: University of the North.
Mulemfo, M.M. 2000. *Thabo Mbeki and the African Renaissance*. Pretoria: Actua Press.
Mutabazi, E. 2002. 'Preparing African Leaders'. In *Cross-cultural Approaches to Leadership Development*, eds. C.B. Derr, S. Roussillon and F. Bournois, 202–14. Washington, DC: Quorum Books.
Oosthuizen, G.C. 1985. 'Africa's Social and Cultural Heritage in a New Era'. *Journal of Contemporary African Studies – Special Jubilee Edition*: 77–113.
Rasheed, S. and D. Olowu (eds.). 1993. *Ethics and Accountability in African Public Services*. Addis Ababa: AAPAM.
Setiloane, G.M. 1988. *African Theology: An Introduction*. Pretoria: Skotaville.
Stayt, H.A. 1968. *The Bavenda*. London: Frank Cass.
Thompson, P. 1978. *The Voice of the Past: Oral History*. Oxford: Oxford University Press.

Tshikwatamba, N.E. 2003. 'African Values in Perspective and the Reconstruction of Bridges for Contextual Development'. Unpublished article.

———. 2004. 'Contextualizing the Guidelines of Public Administration with the Selected African Community Values'. *Journal of Public Administration* 39 (2): 255–71.

Vansina, J. 1965. *Oral Tradition: A Study in Historical Methodology*. Penguin: Harmondsworth.

Zuma, J. 2008. 'Traditional Leaders Here to Stay'. http://www.southafrica.info/what_happening/news/traditionalleaders_120503.htm (accessed 12 February 2008).

7

Africa's Healing Wisdom
Spiritual and Ethical Values of Traditional African Healthcare Practices

LUCINDA DOMOKO MANDA

I ONCE HAD the privilege of listening as two South African women confided in each other. One shared her problems with us. She and her husband had been married for five years and had so far failed to conceive a child by natural means. She had explored all the possible avenues, seeking assistance from both a local physician and a gynecologist. She and her husband had even embarked on expensive fertility treatments, but sadly for them, they still had not managed to conceive a child. It had become evident to this woman that no amount of money spent visiting and consulting with Western-trained doctors had assisted them in their desperate attempts to have a child of their own.

The other woman was sympathetic and offered advice. She had heard of an *isangoma* (traditional healer) who had assisted numerous couples with fertility problems and after consulting with her, these couples had successfully managed to conceive and bear children. The childless woman decided that she had nothing to lose and acting on the advice of her friend, she and her husband visited a traditional healer seeking assistance. The *isangoma* explained the root causes of the couple's infertility. What transpired from the *vumisa* (diagnostic session) was that they had displeased their ancestors and in order for them to be able to conceive a child, they had to ask for forgiveness for past wrongdoings. They were advised to observe some rituals that involved slaughtering a cow. It was a very emotional and cathartic event where the couple asked the ancestors to pardon them for any transgressions they may have committed and to help them conceive a child. A few months after the ceremony, my friend and I went to visit the woman again and were welcomed with the wonderful news that she was pregnant.

Of course, there could be many explanations. The causes for this joyful culmination might be medical, psychological, or simply happy coincidence. My point is only that given the worldview held by this woman, her condition of childlessness and subsequent pregnancy were set into a context of meaning, which enabled her to make sense of these events. Consequently, she and her husband had already decided on the name '*Jabulani*', which means happiness or to be happy.

Introduction

This chapter seeks to investigate the value of African traditional healthcare practices and systems by exploring how the traditional African worldview, its ethics and healthcare practices, serve women in search of social, spiritual and physical healing. The story above makes it clear that in some instances, Western medicine, physicians, gynecologists, etc., are not always able to attend to the problems of Africans. Indeed, the point that we many glean from this story is that the over-specialised, mechanistic worldview that sometimes marks Western medicine, which excludes spiritual and relational issues, is inadequate for everybody. Therefore there are important things to be learned from traditional African approaches to healing, even for those who do not share the specific African cosmology.

The perceived inadequacy of Western healthcare is often associated with a purely functionalistic or mechanistic approach in which healing methods aim solely at isolating and treating the medical problem. In African healing practices, by contrast, a holistic approach to health is key. In this context, healing methods involve not only a recovery from bodily ailments, but also a social, spiritual and psychological reintegration of the patient into the community of the living and the living-dead. This is strongly predicated on the principle of *ubuntu*, the foundational doctrine of traditional African ethics that emphasises that a person is a person through others. Since everyday life is filled with uncertainty, relationships formed with others in the physical and metaphysical or spiritual realm offer a feeling of security.

With this in mind, the first part of this chapter discusses the perceived inadequacy of Western medicine. I seek to explain and give reasons why, in a modern world, many Africans continue to believe in the efficacy of traditional African healthcare practices and systems. African conceptualisations of health and illness, disease and healing are discussed, which are linked to a broader framework of the traditional African worldview. The aim here is to show differences between Western and African healthcare practices and systems.

The second part of this chapter discusses whether medical pluralism is achievable in Africa. There is no doubt that Western medicine based on Western scientific methods has been highly effective in combating disease and illness in Africa. Yet, in some instances, it is inadequately prepared to deal with Africans' health problems. Accepting a dual healthcare system is important since the values and ethical traditions that accompany traditional African medicine and healing practices are useful. These arguments are presented in light of the fact that strong beliefs in Africa's healing wisdom are still prevalent today and are respected by many Africans.

The third part of this chapter examines what the implications such an approach will have on what I refer to as the 'two landscapes of healing' in Africa. It is argued that an inclusive approach to healthcare in which the two systems of healthcare no longer stand parallel to each other, but are side by side is what should be encouraged. I emphasise this simply because such an approach to healthcare will help to eradicate competition between the two systems and to reduce suspicions of Africa's traditional healing wisdom. What will hopefully emerge is a system that seeks to integrate Western and African healthcare practices in ways that they complement and understand each other's practices. The benefits accrued from accepting the value and usefulness of African traditional rituals and medicine will ensure that Africa's healing wisdom will be taken seriously and afforded space in medical discourse.

The inadequacy of Western medicine and healing practices among Africans

> When practices, rituals and customs in African traditional culture are discussed most people from Western societies view traditional Africa as much less developed, even primitive. When studying traditional medical practices in Africa one sees that they seem, at first, ineffective and based only on superstition. However, the

common mistake that Westerners make is trying to view traditional African societies from a contemporary Western perspective. (Mungazi 1996, 71)

Prior to and during colonial times, thinking, writing and analysis on the subject of Africans in general and later, on the subject of African traditional healthcare systems and healing rituals, have always been through the lenses of outsiders: Western missionaries, colonialists and anthropologists. These groups of people have unapologetically denigrated Africa's healing wisdom and heritage as primitive and have often been inclined to be too quick to pass judgement on the cultural practices of Africans, without looking first to understand them. This is primarily because these outsiders have compared African medical practitioners and healthcare practices to their Western counterparts. Upon encountering a traditional healer, writers from the West often misunderstood the role that traditional healers play in the healing of African patients and wrongly called them 'witch-doctors', who practised black magic simply because an aura of mysticism surrounded the healing rituals (Mbiti 1970, 218). For example, Henri Philippe Junod, in his book *Bantu Heritage*, in some instances, passes judgement on the medical practices of Africans, without attempting to understand the processes: 'A Bantu doctor has no stethoscope and no idea about proper auscultation. He uses his eyes a little, but his chief means of diagnosis is divination with his "bones".' Junod further expresses how he feels about the art of 'bone throwing' and states, 'It is difficult to persuade [Africans] that the principle underlying the system entirely wrong and unscientific, being purely magic' (1938, 114).

Such statements demonstrate that Westerners often have difficulty in grasping the cultural practices of Africans and as a result, 'tend to impose their own beliefs upon a group of people who have retained their cultural values for generations and regard them as primitive simply because those values have been maintained for an extended period of time' (Mbiti 1970, 218). Perhaps it is because, as Stephen Owoahene-Acheampong writes, 'The traditional (narrow) Western views of health and healing have been determined by the Western (capitalist) worldview of which they form a part. They are rooted in a worldview which is limited by its individualistic, rationalistic, and materialistic approach to things' (1998, 121). Or as Makinde remarks: 'To the Western mind which believes only in Western science and medicine, science is purely physical and empirical'. It is, possibly, 'for this reason that the Western mind finds African medicine, either impossible or just too fantastic to believe' (1988, 98–99).

This outlook on the world and life is reflected in Western societies and therefore in institutions of medicine that employ Western-trained medical practitioners. A hospital, for example, has many wards – a pediatric ward, a maternity ward, a psychiatric ward, etc. Each ward and its doctors function and exist independently of one another. Consequently, the human being is split into body, mind and soul, and healing is undertaken according to the area of expertise of the particular medical practitioner.

So the Western medical paradigm 'views disease and illness as physical or mechanical disorders with little relationship with a person's social and religious experiences' (Sindiga 1995, 22). In other words, disease and illness are viewed as anomalies or abnormalities caused by diet, genes, cell and viral irregularities, all of which explain biological conditions without any regard given to social conditions. This is because Western medicine is predicated on scientific and experimental or empirical medical theory that seeks to 'divide the body into systems and compartments and measures functions by evaluating tissues and examining fluids' (Pal 2002, 519). Abnormalities in cell structures and the proliferation of viruses in the body are therefore examined, diagnosed and treated. Since the disease or illness is conceived as separate from all other departments of an individual's life, treatment is 'restricted to controlling and eliminating physical symptoms' that afflict the patient (Sindiga 1995, 22). The patient is seen merely as an individual who harbours a germ or foreign organism that needs to be isolated and treated in order to restore his or her health.

This is not the case in traditional Africa. The traditional healer operates much like a general practitioner or a family doctor whose practice is not oriented to specific medical expertise, but instead covers a variety of medical problems in patients of all ages and all conditions. Over time, a general practitioner will come to know his or her patients on an intimate level and much the same can be said about a traditional healer. Since every village or community has or knows of a traditional healer to whom people regularly pay visits, the healer also becomes the friend, pastor, psychiatrist and doctor of traditional African villages and communities (Mbiti 1970, 223).

Where the traditional healer differs from the general practitioner is that he or she holds no degrees or titles and uses no scientific instruments;

rather he or she inspires confidence because the approach to medicine and medical treatment is holistic, in the sense that all aspects of the patient's life are examined – mind, body and soul – in order to determine the root causes of the problem. The traditional healer has to 'discover the cause of the sickness, find out who the criminal is, diagnose the nature of the disease, apply the right treatment, and supply a means of preventing the misfortune from occurring again'. This process of identifying the cause of illness is 'partly psychological and partly physical' (Mbiti 1970, 221). Once the problem has been identified, the healer applies both physical and spiritual (or psychological) treatment, which assures the sufferer that all is and will be well. In short, the treatment process goes beyond addressing the symptoms of disease to discovering its deep-seated causes and subsequently discovering ways of preventing it from recurring. In this manner, there is an effort made towards the psychological, social, and spiritual reintegration of the patient into a state of health and well-being.

Western medicine often lacks a spiritual component and is 'founded in part on materialism' (Bujo 2001, 97). Materialism, in this context 'refers to the theory that physical matter is the only or fundamental reality, and that all beings and processes and phenomena are manifestations or results of matter' (Hammond-Tooke 1989, 145). Western medicine takes as its starting point the material causation of illness in order to treat the illness and excludes any explanation that 'goes beyond the apparent real world, by ignoring as irrelevant any theory that postulates an intervention in the inexorable workings of the laws of nature from outside the system and examines the body in purely mechanistic terms'. Illness and health are 'seen in terms of relations between the sub-structures of the body. The connections made are scientific, in that they are conceived of in terms of such scientific concepts as overload, heat transfer, virus subdivision, serum levels, chemical imbalance, and so on' (Hammond-Tooke 1989, 145).

In contrast, African traditional medicine seeks more fundamental causes of the distress; often what might be termed religious causes. Mbiti reminds us that Africans are 'notoriously' religious and it is within the traditional religious system that African theories of how illness and disease manifest themselves are often explained. Religion and religious beliefs comprise a strong element in traditional backgrounds and exercise probably greatest influence upon the thinking and living of the people concerned. Religion for African people cannot be divorced from medicine, morality and law:

Because traditional religions permeate all the departments of life, there is no formal distinction between the sacred and the secular, between the religious and non-religious, between the spiritual and the material areas of life. Wherever the African is, there is his religion: he carries it to the fields where he is sowing seeds or harvesting a new crop; he takes it with him to the beer party or to attend a funeral ceremony; and if he is educated, he takes religion with him to the examination room at school or in the university; if he is a politician he takes it to the house of parliament. (Mbiti 1970, 2)

For example, when an African is gravely ill, a question that surfaces eventually in the patient's mind is *who* is causing the illness, or *who* has sent it (Hammond-Tooke 1989, 149). Even when it is explained to the patient 'he has malaria because a mosquito carrying malaria parasites stung him he will still want to know why that mosquito stung him and not another person' (Mbiti 1970, 222). Since Africans are curious to know the cause of illness, the explanations offered take into account the patient's environment and social relations. This is why in some cases traditional healers explain illness as caused by, for example, failure to respect elders, a failure to perform rituals that appease the ancestors, or a lack of good behavior to kith or kin.

There are, of course, dangers in this approach. The desire to know who is to blame for an illness or misfortune easily leads to victimisation of innocents branded as witches. African tradition is right in seeking to place illness into a pattern of meaning, a pattern that goes beyond a merely mechanistic explanation. But, as will be argued later, a complementary recognition of the insights of Western science may help to combat what would otherwise be unhelpful and misleading superstition. The recommendations given, or the treatment supplied must therefore take into account the person's social, psychological and spiritual relations.

The inability of Western medicine to provide explanations of why individuals have fallen sick to some extent affirms why there is a feeling of inadequacy of Western medicine among Africans. It is clear from the above discussion that the Western doctor and the African patient use 'different values systems and frames of reference leading to the disillusionment of the patient with the treatment process' (Sindiga 1995, 22). Thus we can comprehend why many Africans still tend to turn to African traditional healers when Western medicine fails to inspire confidence in its healing methods.

The African conceptualisation of health and healing

The Western views of health and the medical procedures followed in the search for healing are, as noted above, markedly different from the procedures Africans follow and relate to when in search of a medical cure. It is apparent that the differences in the practice of medicine and the healing methods that accompany the consultative process emanate from and are moulded or shaped by a particular worldview. The traditional African worldview, unlike the mainstream Western worldview, conceptualises life holistically and this holistic approach towards life filters through all other aspects namely health, illness, and healing.

In general, among Africans and African women in particular, health is very important in many ways and for various reasons. Maintaining one's health is vital because 'health is viewed in terms of the ability of an individual to fulfill his or her responsibilities in the community' (Owoahene-Acheampong 1998, 122). For women in particular, their health and strength is essential for the survival of the community. It is well known that women are the caregivers, nurturers, farmers and homemakers of the family. Their ability to fulfil their day-to-day chores hinges on whether they are well or unwell.

Productivity, in this respect, 'has a very important place in African conceptions of health' (Owoahene-Acheampong 1998, 122). Obligations to the community and individual members must, therefore, be carried out since the underlying attitude towards other people is survival. To ensure survival, each individual must be consciously aware that they depend on one another. In other words, there is a strong aura of reciprocity between people, which acknowledges that 'the well-being of a person depends upon his or her fellow men and women in the group' (1998, 123). It is no exaggeration, therefore, when Mbiti expressively says of Africans,

> Only in terms of other people does the individual become conscious of his own being, his own duties, his privileges and responsibilities towards himself and towards other people. When he suffers, he does not suffer alone but with his corporate group: when he rejoices, he rejoices not alone but with his kinsmen, his neighbours and his

relatives whether dead or living... whatever happens to the individual happens to the whole group, and whatever happens to the whole group happens to the individual. The individual can only say, 'I am, because we are; and since we are, therefore, I am'. (1970, 141)

We return to *ubuntu*. The principle of 'I am, because we are; and since we are, therefore, I am', or in isiZulu, '*Umuntu ngumuntu ngabantu*', validates the idea that a person is a person through others. This idiom suggests that the well-being of a person is only possible through the community and the web of relationships that are formed from being part of a community. Furthermore, this maxim shows that the traditional African ethos is such that 'one cannot regard even one's own life as purely personal property or concern. It is the group which is the owner of life, a person being just a link in the chain uniting the present and future generations' (Kasenene 2000, 349).

Reproductive health is also very important to the African conception of health and the story at the beginning of this chapter captures this clearly, as it is made clear that women have a responsibility to bear children. Women, as Isabel Phiri notes, are 'sacred vessels of life' (1997, 70) and so it is expected that the woman, as a symbol of fertility, will carry out the task of bringing life into the world. Her function and position in African families and communities is thus affirmed by her ability to pass on life. The ability to conceive and bring children into the world is cherished and is also indicative that the individual is well. An inability to conceive sends a clear message that all is not well. The danger in this type of approach is that the responsibility of barrenness is laid solely on the woman's shoulders and it does not attempt to take into consideration that perhaps it is the husband who is infertile. Moreover, if people hold the belief that childless women are witches, this perception can allow for the persecution of innocent women, thus avoiding establishing the actual cause of childlessness. For African women, their ability to have children is a reflection of the health of the parents and, as 'the extension of self', is a way of guaranteeing a future (Owoahene-Acheampong 1998, 124). The guarantee for a future here means that the danger of extinction is prevented since in the traditional African worldview, one is perceived as 'cut off' or 'disconnected', if one has not left anyone behind. Parents wish to ensure that they will have descendants who can perform duties towards their ancestors in order to keep the memory of those who have passed on, and thus the living-dead, alive.

Being healthy is also a reflection of correct harmony or balance between persons, the natural environment and the spiritual world. The natural environment and the people are all understood to possess intrinsic worth. Hence respect for the environment warrants the need to preserve it and to view it as a sacred entity that exists independently of men and women. This approach to health that takes into consideration the natural and the supernatural elements is holistic and therefore the ethical imperative is not to treat the natural world as a means to an end, but as an end in itself, since 'the other' or nature is also part of the self (Sindima 1995, 127). This view of the Earth differs sharply from the dominant view held by Western capitalism that drives the idea of productivity spurring on new patterns of consumerism or consumption and in the process generating capital accumulation.

Can medical pluralism be achieved?

A critical question: Can and should medical pluralism exist in the light of the fact that different people who hold different cultural backgrounds understand and conceptualise health and healing rather differently to other cultural groups? The answer and argument presented in this chapter is a resounding 'yes'. Western medicine, within its own paradigm, has had a huge and positive impact upon world health, particularly in combating viruses, malaria, polio and the like. In addition, most Africans have to some extent been Westernised in their views and outlook.

The colonial interface in Africa undoubtedly altered the African landscape and the traditional values and belief systems of Africans. Colonialism not only altered these traditions, but also sought to systematically remove and replace them with European or Western values, ethics and ideologies that espoused capitalism, individualism and materialism, thus stripping away the pride of traditional African practices. Consequently, what Africa and Africans inherited from the West 'undermined or even disrupted, to some degree, the traditional ethos' (Kasenene 2000, 348). However, not all was lost and not all was replaced. In fact, most of Africa's rich heritage of traditional beliefs still persists and is still relevant and readily available to Africans who choose to access and subscribe to aspects of African tradition.

Such is the case made for traditional African medicine, values, ethics and healing systems.

It is thus gratifying that in most African countries, for instance, two medical systems exist, albeit parallel to each other. On the one hand, there is the modern and highly institutionalised Western medical system and alongside or parallel to this, there is the traditional and un-institutionalised African medical system. As a result, an African who requires medical attention is 'spoilt for choice' and 'has available both Western-trained physicians and indigenous healers' (Ngubane 1992, 366). Quite often Africans make use of both traditional and modern medicine, either at the same time for the same episode of illness, or separately for different illnesses.

The shift between the 'two landscapes of healing' is dependent on what the patients view as the main cause of ill health. If they believe, for example, that illness such as dysentery, diarrhoea, rheumatism in older people, or a skin rash in children is caused naturally, they may be treated either by modern medicine, or by traditional medicine, or by both. On the other hand, if they believe that an illness is caused by human-induced forces such as sorcery, witchcraft, spiritual disturbances, or breaching socio-religious obligations and taboos, especially with regard to their ancestors, such afflictions will be referred to traditional healers (Sindiga 1995, 20).

For example, barrenness or female infertility is believed to be best handled by traditional healers because the inability to conceive 'implies God's punishment for some kind of wrongdoing that requires appropriate expiation under the direction of professional priests, priestesses, diviners, or others' (Paris 1995, 79). A childless marriage is interpreted as constituting a 'major moral and spiritual problem for all concerned'. The story at the beginning of this chapter supports the view that female infertility indicates a major moral transgression that needs to be corrected on a spiritual level by a traditional healer. The fact that the woman was able to conceive after a referral to a traditional healer gives strong testimony that traditional African medical healthcare practices and systems are valuable. The Western-trained physician was unable to interrogate the spiritual and social relations of the patient simply because the evaluation methods used are different. In this respect, I argue that in Africa much emphasis must be placed on affording generous space to accommodating indigenous healing systems, as they play a pivotal role in primary healthcare.

The implications of 'two landscapes of healing' in Africa

M.V. Gumede, a Western-trained medical doctor, accurately notes that the broad aims of both traditional and modern healers are in essence directed towards healing patients who are sick. 'Both modern healers and traditional healers have the same goal, namely, to help the sick and ill-at-ease. The aim is to cure the illness if they can ... If not, to relieve pain and suffering which both often do, but also, to comfort the sufferer and the relatives' (1990, 153). No doubt this is the central goal of anyone in the health profession, in which the desires and goals are to cure illness in order to preserve and sustain life. The obligation of healthcare workers is therefore clear, irrespective of the means used in order to achieve that end. In short, both traditional and modern healers place the needs of the patient first.

While it is clear that they share a common goal, it should be noted that each system of medicine has its own strengths and weaknesses, such that one cannot entirely dominate the other. This is especially true in areas where illness is perceived to take on a spiritual dimension. For example, African traditional medicine is perhaps superior to Western allopathic medicine when it comes to addressing and responding to issues concerning a patient experiencing the urge or calling to become a diviner or herbalist. Vera Bührmann recounts an incident of a traditional healing ceremony that brought change in the life of a woman who was successful in business and started developing aliments that would not respond to allopathic treatment:

> For many years she worked as a successful businesswoman and not as a healer. She became obese and developed asthma and depression, and medication made no difference. Then her children transgressed an unpardonable family taboo. This forced her to arrange a big *inthlombe* (a song and dance session). It was a very emotional event where she asked the pardon of the ancestors and relatives and clan members. This was a turning point in her life. She returned to her practice as a healer, lost weight and got rid of her asthma. When seen a year later she was happy and had a busy practice. (1996, 124)

This example demonstrates aspects of the strength of African traditional healing systems that Western medicine cannot deal with, or address successfully. Many Africans would identify with this woman and interpret the efficacy of African traditional medicine, as opposed to Western medicine, as the inability of Western medicine to interrogate the spiritual and social dimension of disease.

The most serious deficit in Western medicine from an African perspective is that it usually fails to treat and examine patients' social relationships with both the living and the living-dead. On the other hand, traditional healers do not usually possess the knowledge and technological expertise to deal with viruses (especially HIV), tuberculosis, glaucoma, cerebral malaria or many of the other illnesses and diseases common in Africa (although they may often be able to provide significant help with secondary effects). Nor are they able to offer surgical procedures that may make the difference between life and death for a patient. Yet despite the differences between the two healing systems, it is apparent that where one fails, the other takes over. The two systems of healthcare are complementary. Hence I argue that a mutually respectful and symbiotic relationship between the two should be strongly encouraged, supported and developed.

What are the implications of the 'two landscapes of healing' in Africa, particularly for Africans? The inclusion of both practices of medicine will ensure that interaction between the two is possible. Communication channels will open up that will eventually lead to co-operation. This will then foster and encourage the exchange of knowledge and information between the 'two landscapes of healing'. In essence, it will allow for Western-trained medical doctors to acquire a basic understanding of ideas and notions of disease and illness that African patients understand and relate to. This would further assist them in understanding the social and cultural views that define disease and illness, given that African patients use different frames of reference and value-systems with regard to diagnosing, managing and treating illnesses. It may also help Western-trained health professionals to understand why their patients prefer to seek traditional help before seeking Western forms of healthcare. If the two medical systems arrive at the point where a mutual respect for each other's work exists, they will then begin to appreciate that they share similar goals: to heal and cure the sick. Once interpreted in this manner, both the Western-trained doctors and the African traditional healers will begin to accept one another and not view each other as competitors. When this is achieved, 'the superior-inferior culture complex that pervades attitudes toward recognition of traditional or indigenous medical systems' (Gumede 1990, 227) will fall away. What will hopefully emerge in its place to replace such antiquated attitudes is one common vision: health for all.

Conclusion

Martin Luther King once remarked, 'If we are going to go forward, we must go back and rediscover those precious values – that all reality hinges on moral foundations and that all reality has spiritual control' (1999, 33). This is essentially what I have set out to suggest in this chapter: that there is value in Africa's healing wisdom that serves a purpose for many African men and women.

Africa's healing wisdom rests on the moral principles that are espoused in African traditional religions. The concept of *ubuntu*, the primary principle of traditional African ethics that emphasises the relatedness and connection between the physical and metaphysical world serves as the basis of how Africans understand concepts of disease, sickness, and health. This ethical principle is consequently applied to African traditional healing rituals and medicine and sets guidelines for interrogating the causes and social dimensions of health, disease and sickness. This approach to healthcare, as I have shown, is holistic, since social and cultural dimensions of health are incorporated into the diagnosis of the illness. This is what is often lacking in the Western approach to health and healing. While it is accepted that Western medicine has served and continues to serve the needs of African people and I do not dispute the important role it plays in providing healthcare, it is also strongly recommended that we must accept that it is not superior. It does not have all the answers, since it does not interrogate all aspects of a person's life. On this basis, I argue that the government and healthcare professionals, both traditional and modern healers, should strive towards building a complementary working relationship between the two systems. To bring this position full circle, the story at the beginning of this chapter, in part, pays testimony to the need for co-operation. The couple would have not wasted time and resources on Western healthcare if African healthcare systems were immediately perceived as relevant.

Select bibliography

Bührmann, M.V. 1996. 'Views of Healing and the Healer'. In *Cultural Synergy in South Africa: Weaving Strands of Africa and Europe*, eds. M. Steyn and K. Motshabi, 119–30. Randburg: Knowledge Resources.

Bujo, B. 2001. *Foundations of an African Ethic: Beyond the Universal Claims of Western Morality*. New York: Crossroad.

Gumede, M.V. 1990. *Traditional Healers: A Medical Doctor's Perspective*. Braamfontein: Stokaville.

Hammond-Tooke, D. 1989. *Rituals and Medicines*. Johannesburg: A.D. Donker.

Junod, H.P. 1938. *Bantu Heritage*. Johannesburg: Hortors.

Kasenene, P. 2000. 'African Ethical Theory and the Four Principles'. In *Cross-cultural Perspectives in Medical Ethics*, ed. R.M. Veatch, 347–57. Sudbury, Massachusetts: Jones and Bartlett.

King, Jr., M.L. 1999. *The Autobiography of Martin Luther King, Jr*. Ed. C. Carson. London: Little Brown.

Makinde, M.A. 1988. *African Philosophy, Culture and Traditional Medicine*. Ohio: Ohio University Press.

Mbiti, J.S. 1970. *African Religions and Philosophies*. New York: Anchor Books.

Mungazi, D.A. 1996. *Gathering under the Mango Tree*. New York: Peter Lang.

Ngubane, H. 1992. 'Clinical Practice and Organization of Indigenous Healers in South Africa'. In *The Social Basis of Health and Healing in Africa*, eds. S. Feierman and J. Janzen, 366–75. Berkeley: University of California Press.

Owoahene-Acheampong, S. 1998. *Inculturation and African Religion: Indigenous and Western Approaches to Medical Practice*. New York: Peter Lang.

Pal, S.K. 2002. 'Complementary and Alternative Medicine: An Overview'. *Current Science* 82 (5), 10 March: 518–24.

Paris, P. 1995. *The Spirituality of African Peoples: The Search for a Common Moral Discourse*. Minneapolis: Fortress.

Phiri, I. 1997. 'Doing Theology in Community: The Case of African Women Theologians in the 1990s'. *Journal of Theology for Southern Africa* 99: 68–90.

Sindiga, I. 1995. 'African Ethnomedicine and Other Medical Systems'. In *Traditional Medicine in Africa*, eds. I. Sindiga, C. Nyaigotti-Chacha and M.P. Kanunah, 16–29. Nairobi: East African Educational Publishers.

Sindima, H.J. 1995. *Africa's Agenda: The Legacy of Liberalism and Colonialism in the Crisis of African Values*. Connecticut: Greenwood Press.

Contributors

DR EZRA CHITANDO is one of the leading scholars in the field of African religion. He teaches at the University of Zimbabwe.

LUCINDA DOMOKO MANDA is from Malawi and a doctoral student in the School of Philosophy and Ethics at the University of KwaZulu-Natal. She researches in the field of African ethics, with special emphasis on issues affecting women and women's health in Africa.

PROFESSOR JOHN MTYUWAFHETHU MAFUNISA is a member of the Department of Public Administration and Management at the University of South Africa. He is deputy editor and chairperson of the editorial committee for the *Journal of Public Administration*.

PROFESSOR NHLANHLA MKHIZE is deputy-head of the School of Psychology at the University of KwaZulu-Natal. His research has been on the relationship between traditional African beliefs and philosophy and Western psychological models.

DR MUNYARADZI FELIX MUROVE is a senior lecturer in the School of Philosophy and Ethics at the University of KwaZulu-Natal. He is currently editing an anthology of African ethics from a comparative and applied perspective.

DR RONALD NICOLSON is a retired professor of Religious Studies and former Dean of Human and Management Sciences on the Pietermaritzburg campus of the former University of Natal.

DR NEVILLE RICHARDSON was an academic in the School of Religion and Theology at the University of KwaZulu-Natal for 25 years. He is now the principal of John Wesley College and director of the Education for Ministry and Mission Unit of the Methodist Church of southern Africa.

PROFESSOR AUGUSTINE SHUTTE is a member of the Philosophy Department at the University of Cape Town. His most recent research has been in the field of science and religion and he has published a collection of papers called *The Quest for Humanity in Science and Religion: The South African Experience*.

Index

abuse, sexual 60 *see also* gender inequality; women, status
Adedeji, A. 98–99
African Ethics Initiative 1, 12
Africanisation 107
Africanness 81
aid dependence 105
ancestors 10, 36–37, 48–49, 58, 80, 120–22, 125, 131, 134–37
apartheid 16, 33, 66–67, 72–77, 81, 111, 119
Aquinas, T. 10, 19–20, 23–24 *see also* Thomism/Thomists
avarice 95

Bewaji, J.A.I. 49
Bible 18–19, 76
Black Consciousness 77
black economic empowerment (BEE) 107
Bleek, W. 8
Boon, M. 103–04
Botswana, HIV/AIDS 45
Bujo, B. 49, 56, 58, 59, 89–90, 94–95, 130
ubuntu 1, 5–6, 8–10, 33, 35–43, 57, 65–68, 78–82, 107, 112, 114–17, 121, 126, 133, 138
business practices 98

capitalism 11–12, 95, 99–100, 134
  African 103, 107
  Western 86–108

caregiving 45–46, 53–54, 58–60 *see also* PLWHA
Christianity/Christians 4, 7, 11, 20, 47, 56, 58, 59–60, 66, 80, 82, 98, 121–22
churches
  African 97
  Anglican 4
  Catholic 24, 49
  Episcopalian 4
collectivism 95, 114
colonialism 33, 79, 87, 89–90, 95, 102, 107, 114, 121, 134
communalism 27–28, 39, 41, 57, 87, 89–91, 94–95, 98, 104–07, 112–15
Communism 86, 93
condoms 53, 55, 58
Constitution, South Africa, 1996 65–66, 70, 118, 121
corruption 3, 6, 91, 115
creative power 37–38, 103
culture, African values 87, 107, 122–23, 128 *see also* religion; tradition, African

deontology 21–22
De Soto, H. 99–100
disease 39, 54, 129–30, 137–38 *see also* healthcare
diviners 120, 135–36
Dube, M. 51, 54

economics
  African   86–87, 90, 94, 97–99, 103
  anthropological   100–03
empiricism   21
Enlightenment   72–73
ethics
  African   1–13, 16–17, 23, 32–34, 35–43, 48–49, 59, 103, 125–26, 135, 138
  European   16–23, 134
  definition   46, 112
  global   4–5, 10, 13, 15
  and religion   45–50, 56–58, 60–61
  sexual   58

family   28, 114
fertility/infertility   125, 133, 135
First World   15, 16
free enterprise   97, 101
freedom   24, 33, 113
frugality   95–96

gender inequality   51–52, 55–56, 59
  see also masculinities; women
Gerwel, J.   68–73, 75–76
global village   2–5, 15
globalisation   15–34, 79, 82
God   18–19, 36–38, 40, 48–49, 66–67
gold   89
Grinker, R.R.   102–03
Gyekye, K.   48–49, 106–07

Hammond-Tooke, D.   130–31
harambee   12, 105–07
harmony   38–39
healing, social   69, 71–77
healthcare see also disease
  African   125–38
  Western   125–32, 134–38
Hegel, G.   23
HIV/AIDS   11, 45–46, 50–60, 137
Hobbes, T.   39, 71

homo oeconomicus   102
homosexuality   4, 52
human nature   17, 23, 30–33
human relationships   25–26, 30, 36, 43, 73, 102, 126, 133
human rights   66
humanisation   103–07
humanism   49, 104–05, 108
humanity   18–19, 23, 25, 28, 37, 68, 90
Hume, D.   21
Hunter, G.   95–96

indigenisation   107
individualism   93–94, 134
Islam   4, 7, 11, 96–97, 121

Jesus Christ   19, 60
Junod, H.P.   128

Kant, I.   21, 23
Karenga, M.   36–42
Kasenene, P.   46–48
Kaunda, K.   116–17
Kennedy, P.   97–98
Kenyata, J.   94, 105–06
Khoi people   7–8
Kierkegaard, S.   23

labour   12, 88–90, 96, 105
  communal   90, 116
land ownership   86–87, 99
Lapin, D.   114–15
law   19–20, 39
leaders, traditional   118
Lloyd, L.   8

Maat   10, 36, 39–43
Malthus, T.   92
Maluleke, T.S.   53, 73–78, 81
Mamdani, M.   74–75
Mandela, N.   3–4, 76–78
Mandeville, B.   91–92
Marx, K.   92–93, 100

masculinities 11, 45, 50–60 *see also* gender inequality
Mashiri, P. 55
materialism 130, 134
Mauss, M. 100–01
Mazrui, A. 12, 87–88, 90–91, 95, 98, 103
Mbigi, I. 115–16
Mbiti, J.S. 40, 46–47, 120–21, 130–33
medicine *see* healthcare
Menkiti, I.A. 27
morality 18–21, 30–32, 35, 37, 46–49, 58, 82, 113, 120–21
Mugabe, R. 3, 52
umuntu (person) 29, 32–33, 40–42

narratives 72–73
Nujoma, S. 52
Nyerere, J. 3, 104–05

Olowu, D. 113, 115
oral tradition 119–20

peace (social) 71–72, 74
philosophy, Greek 24, 32
PLWHA (people living with HIV and AIDS) 53–55, 59
Polanyi, K. 101–02
poverty 92, 95
  alleviation 106
prestige motive 90–95, 98, 102
productivity 105, 114, 122, 132
profit motive 89–95, 102
public service 112, 118, 120, 122

Rahner, K. 24
rape 55, 60
Rasheed, S. 113, 115
rationalism 21
reconciliation 65, 67, 69–77, 81–82
  see also Truth and Reconciliation Commission

religion *see also* culture, African values; tradition, African
  African 6–7, 46–48, 60, 106–07, 112, 120–22
  and disease 130–31
  and HIV/AIDS 45–46
Renaissance, African 114, 122

Samkange, M. 90
Samkange, S. 90
San people 7–8
isangoma 8, 125
science 20–22, 24–25, 32
self-determination 25–27, 30
self-help projects 115
self-realisation 25–27, 31
Senghor, L. 27–28
seriti 6, 8–10, 27, 29–30, 32
Setiloane, G.M. 29–30, 113
Shire, C. 55
slavery 88
Smith, A. 92
socialism 95, 107
solidarity 56–61, 101
spiritualism, African 121–22
Steiner, C.B. 102–03
stokvels 115

'Takers' 103–04
theology 76–77
Third World 15, 16, 98
  Africa 16, 103–04
Thomism/Thomists 25–27, 30–32
  see also Aquinas, T.
Thompson, P. 119
tradition, African 27–30, 82, 86–87, 90, 97, 103–04, 106, 112–14, 117–20, 134 *see also* culture, African values; healthcare; religion
Truth and Reconciliation Commission (TRC) 4, 11, 17, 65–77, 80–81, 118–19

amnesty 66, 73–74
reparation 73
Tshikwatamba, N.E. 114, 121–22
Tutu, *Archbishop* D. 11, 66–68, 71, 76–78, 81

Union of South Africa, 1910 70
unity
  cosmic 38
  national 69–72, 75
utilitarianism 22

values, African 112–15
Van Binsbergen, W. 11, 78–81
Van Onselen, C. 97
virtues 17–18

wealth 92, 94, 96–99, 104–05

Weber, M. 88, 96–97, 117
Whitehead, A.N. 93, 100
Wiredu, K. 48–49, 106
witches/witchcraft 80, 94, 131, 133, 135
women *see also* gender inequality
  child-bearers 125, 133–35
  carriers of disease 55
  status 11, 51–52, 55, 59–60, 132
work ethic 12, 88–90, 96, 111–12, 115, 122–23

Zambia 116
Zhakata, L. 55
Zimbabwe
  HIV/AIDS 45, 52–53, 55
  women, status 55
Zuma, J. 118